Deep Learning for Engineers

Deep Learning for Engineers introduces the fundamental principles of deep learning along with an explanation of the basic elements required for understanding and applying deep learning models.

As a comprehensive guideline for applying deep learning models in practical settings, this book features an easy-to-understand coding structure using Python and PyTorch with an in-depth explanation of four typical deep learning case studies on image classification, object detection, semantic segmentation, and image captioning. The fundamentals of convolutional neural network (CNN) and recurrent neural network (RNN) architectures and their practical implementations in science and engineering are also discussed.

This book includes exercise problems for all case studies focusing on various fine-tuning approaches in deep learning. Science and engineering students at both undergraduate and graduate levels, academic researchers, and industry professionals will find the contents useful.

Deep Learning
for Engineers

Tariq M. Arif
Md Adilur Rahim

CRC Press
Taylor & Francis Group
Boca Raton London New York

CRC Press is an imprint of the
Taylor & Francis Group, an **informa** business

A CHAPMAN & HALL BOOK

First edition published 2024
by CRC Press
2385 NW Executive Center Drive, Suite 320, Boca Raton FL 33431

and by CRC Press
4 Park Square, Milton Park, Abingdon, Oxon, OX14 4RN

CRC Press is an imprint of Taylor & Francis Group, LLC

© 2024 Tariq M. Arif and Md Adilur Rahim

ISBN: 9781032504735 (hbk)
ISBN: 9781032515816 (pbk)
ISBN: 9781003402923 (ebk)

DOI: 10.1201/9781003402923

Typeset in Minion
by KnowledgeWorks Global Ltd.

Access the Instructor and Student Resources/Support Material:
https://www.routledge.com/9781032504735

Contents

About the Authors

Tariq M. Arif is an assistant professor with the Department of Mechanical Engineering at Weber State University, UT. He previously worked at the University of Wisconsin, Platteville, as a lecturer faculty. Tariq obtained his Ph.D. degree in 2017 from the Mechanical Engineering Department of New Jersey Institute of Technology (NJIT), NJ. His main research interests are in the area of artificial intelligence and genetic algorithms for robotics control, computer vision, and biomedical simulations. He completed his Masters in 2011 from the University of Tokushima, Japan, and B.Sc. degree in 2005 from Bangladesh University of Engineering and Technology (BUET). Tariq also worked in the Japanese automobile industry as a CAD/CAE engineer after completing his B.Sc. degree. Throughout his industrial and academic career, Tariq has been involved in many different research projects. At present, he is working on the implementation of deep learning models for various computer vision-based controls and robotics applications.

Md Adilur Rahim is an assistant professor (research) with the Department of Biological and Agricultural Engineering at Louisiana State University Agricultural Center. Rahim completed his Ph.D. degree in 2023 from the Engineering Science program at Louisiana State University, LA. He specializes in flood hazard and risk assessment, natural disaster mitigation, and the application of big data analysis and deep learning techniques. He achieved his M.Sc. degree in Civil Engineering in 2022 from Louisiana State University, LA. Earlier, in 2014, he graduated with a B.Sc. degree in Civil Engineering from the Bangladesh University of Engineering & Technology (BUET). After earning his bachelor's degree, he spent several years as a civil engineer and Agrometeorological data analyst, undertaking major projects with the World Bank in Bangladesh. He has authored numerous peer-reviewed publications in prestigious journals and show-cased his research at several prominent conferences. He has been an active participant in many deep learning projects and competitions, and his works have contributed significantly to the engineering field for solving real-world challenges.

## CHAPTER 1

Introduction

Deep learning is a rapidly growing branch of machine learning that uses many hidden layers to extract features from a large dataset. It is an advanced form of neural network algorithm, where the term "neural" is used to emphasize a learning process comparable to our human brains. Recently, deep learning has seen tremendous growth and achieved significant milestones. This growth and successful implementation of deep learning applications can be attributed to the rise of Graphical Processing Unit (GPU) hardware, readily accessible large data sets, and open source machine learning frameworks. Also, many cloud service providers, such as Amazon Web Service (AWS), Google Cloud Platform, and Microsoft Azure, offer GPU-enabled computing and pay-per-use models, which makes it convenient to develop sophisticated deep learning models. Besides GPU hardware, recently, Tensor Processing Units (TPUs) are also used in many cases for effective and faster deep learning computations. Deep learning-based design has already been used in a wide variety of engineering domains, such as autonomous cars, intelligent robotics, computer vision, natural language processing, and bioinformatics. Additionally, numerous real-world engineering applications can efficiently utilize an existing pre-trained deep learning model that has already been developed and optimized for a related task.

In the last several years, there has also been a surge in academic research on deep learning in almost every domain of science and engineering. Many engineering and manufacturing companies are also competing and investing heavily in deep learning or artificial intelligence-based research. Although a vast amount of information is available online, incorporating

DOI: 10.1201/9781003402923-1

1

a deep learning model in a design/research project is quite challenging, especially for someone who doesn't have related machine learning, GPU dependencies, and cloud computing knowledge. Keeping that in mind, this book is intended to be a practical learning tool for applied deep learning through the example of four different implementation cases.

Some basic knowledge of Python programming is required to follow this book. However, no chapter is devoted to teaching Python programming. Instead, we demonstrated relevant Python commands followed by brief descriptions throughout this book. A common roadblock to exploring the deep learning field by engineering students, researchers, or non-data science professionals is the variation of probabilistic theories and the notations used in data science or computer science books. In order to avoid this complexity, in this book, we mainly focus on the practical implementation part of deep learning theory using Python programming. We assume this approach will make this book interesting and easy to follow. Also, it will give a practical understanding to the reader without going through mathematical details. Another major challenge in exploring deep learning is the GPU configuration and dependency installation tricks in the Pytorch, which require a significant amount of time and effort for newcomers. This unique area is also covered in detail in this book.

Chapter 2 of this book covers fundamental concepts of deep learning from a broader perspective. It also covers important technical terms and their explanations that have been used throughout the case studies presented in Chapters 6–9. The end part of Chapter 2 provides the basics for implementing a transfer learning model in deep learning when a pretrained model is available. Chapter 3 covers the computer vision and Convolutional Neural Network (CNN) fundamentals, its internal parameters, and applications. Chapter 4 covers the basic concepts of natural language processing and Recurrent Neural Network (RNN) architectures. Part of Chapter 4 also covers a short introduction to Generative Adversarial Networks (GANs) models and their applications. However, in the case studies, only the implementations of CNN and RNN are demonstrated.

Chapter 5 demonstrates the procedure, tips, and tricks associated with deep learning framework installation. This chapter outlines how to set up an Nvidia GPU workstation (single or multiple GPU) using PyTorch and CUDA. Chapters 6–9 present the different case studies for deep learning modeling using Python programming. All of these case studies use open-source datasets from Kaggle's site. Chapters 6 shows a case study of an image classification problem, where a deep learning model is trained to classify different road signs (e.g., crosswalk, speed limit, stop sign, traffic light). Chapter 7 shows a case study of object detection, where the model is trained to detect cars on roads. Chapter 8 shows a case study of semantic segmentation using aerial images from a drone. Here, the model is trained to segment the outline of different objects (e.g., car, rock, road, bicycle, etc.). Chapter 9 shows a case study of image captioning, where the model is trained to tell/describe an image using CNN and RNN. Python programming in case studies follows a pattern or structure that is easy to follow (e.g., load library, pre-process dataset, training, etc.). All of the case study chapters are followed by exercise questions that are useful for further fine-tuning the deep learning models and learning hyperparameter tuning. We recommend readers of this book follow the steps shown in Chapter 5 for installing PyTorch and CUDA and apply deep learning models from Chapter 6–9. Readers can also create similar data for their projects and tweak the models and Python codes for specific cases.

The goal of this book is to present simple and easy-to-follow guidelines for deep learning. It is mainly for science and engineering students, researchers, and professionals who wish to explore deep learning models for their projects without having a full journey through machine learning theories. To demonstrate the implementation of deep learning models, it presents four different practical case studies using open-source datasets and software.

## CHAPTER 2

Basics of Deep Learning

2.1 BUILDING BLOCKS

2.1.1 Artificial Neural Networks

An artificial neural network is an algorithm or software architecture that has interconnected layers of functions to learn sophisticated and complex tasks similar to neuron activities in the human brain. Although the process of learning in the human brain is extremely complicated and not fully understood, the software architecture of neural networks uses known activation functions and connected pathways that can be compared to the biological neurons and synapses, respectively. Furthermore, an artificial neural network can learn (i.e., find optimum model weights or biases) through training, which is an important phenomenon that mimics the process of learning in the human brain. For these reasons, the term "Neural" is used in the field of machine learning or deep learning.

Some of the key features of artificial neural network include effective function approximations, identifying patterns, and implementing complex mapping. Recently, it has been used in diverse science, engineering, arts, and medical applications. It is also widely used for forecasting and predicting many real-life businesses, socio-economic issues, remote sensing, biodiversity issues, medical and radiological diagnosis, and much more [1–6]. Artificial neural network architecture has several fundamental building blocks, such as the number of inputs, outputs, hidden layers, and the type of activation functions. A simple multi-layer neural network has a

DOI: 10.1201/9781003402923-2

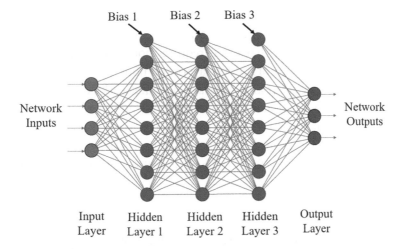

FIGURE 2.1   Multi-layer neural network architecture with three hidden layers.

topology similar to Figure 2.1, which shows a network with one input layer, three hidden layers with biases, and one output layer. Figure 2.1 used the NN-SVG tool partially to generate connected neurons [7]. To train a neural network for meaningful tasks, a dataset is required that has actual or real-life inputs and outputs. For example, a dataset containing information on people's demographic, weight, height, gender, heart rate, alcohol consumption, exercise routine, eating habits, sleep habits, age, etc., can be trained using network inputs (weight, height, gender, heart rate) and network outputs (e.g., age, eating habits). After successful training and validation, if the dataset is large and has good data variations, the model should be able to predict outputs based on similar inputs.

The hidden layers inside a network contain neurons that perform tensor operations based on the output requirements. For example, if our required output is a numerical value, such as predicting body temperature or test score, we use linear regression. On the other hand, we can use logistic regression to predict binary outputs and multiclass outputs. Examples of binary outputs are predicting between true or false, pass or fail, cat or non-cat picture, and examples of multiclass outputs are predicting one class from multiple classes, such as finding out if a picture is a cat, bird, dog, or fish picture. A logistic regression can, however, be used for predicting ordinal outputs (e.g., determining high, medium, or low ranges). During the training process, each input in the neurons is multiplied by weights associated with its connecting pathways and then added to a bias to generate the next output. The outputs from one layer are entered as inputs in the next layer. If an artificial neural network has many hidden layers, it is called deep learning. Therefore, all deep learning networks are a type of artificial neural network that often require more computational powers and have ten to hundreds of hidden layers and nodes.

The learning process of an artificial neural network is actually finding out weights and biases that will generate a minimum error for predicting the required result from a training dataset. The artificial neural network continuously adjusts weights and biases if the network produces poor results. When the network finds the best or desired result, it will no longer update the parameters.

2.1.2 Types of Learning

Through the artificial network, several methods of learning schemes are used based on data types or observation methods, such as supervised, unsupervised, semi-supervised, and reinforcement learning. When the network can compare its predictions with the correct predictions given in the dataset to make adjustments, it is called supervised learning. For example, in computer vision, when a network is trained on a large dataset containing images of different models of cars and then derives a generalized network rule (weights and biases) that can predict a car model from a given image, that is supervised learning. Other examples of supervised learning include stock market forecasting using historical performance data, digital or online marketing based on online browsing data, classifying human emotion based on face images under different circumstances, etc.

Unsupervised learning is the type of learning when the required outputs or correct results from the training dataset are not labeled; that is, the algorithm tries to find key patterns or features without examples. Examples of unsupervised learning include segmenting items in an image without having any training image where similar items have already been segmented, anomaly detection of a machine without having any failure data, etc. In between supervised and unsupervised learning, there is another type of learning called semi-supervised learning. In the case of semi-supervised learning, a dataset is partially labeled, or partial results are given.

Reinforcement learning is another type of learning method that utilizes observations from a complex environment and makes a final decision (output) based on the penalties or reward it received for its performance. The selection of these different types of learning schemes in artificial neural networks depends on the types of datasets and output requirements for a particular task.

2.1.3 Multi-Layer Perceptron

The artificial neural network can learn from training data by going forward and backward (also known as loops) through the network. In this process, the algorithm updates associated weights and biases. A multilayer perceptron (MLP) is a learning algorithm that looks very similar to an artificial neural network; that is, it has multiple layers of classifiers to learn from a labeled dataset. But MLP typically learns through the feedforward process and has the same number of nodes in the hidden layers [8, 9]. It also has at least three sets of fully connected layers: the input layer, hidden layer(s), and output layer. Multiple hidden layers in MLP are suitable for capturing non-linear patterns from labeled data by mapping input values to output values using many simple functions. Generally, MLP is used in supervised learning when the structure of the problem is complex such as in speech recognition and computation linguistics.

2.2 NEURONS AND ACTIVATION FUNCTIONS

There are many parameters inside an artificial neural network that can influence the output. But generally, outputs are directly related to the number of neurons and their activation functions. These neurons are also called artificial neurons or perceptrons, and they are typically shown by circles that are arranged inside the layers. Artificial neuron takes input weights from all connections and adds a bias, initializes these parameters, and then calculates the output using another function known as an activation function. The mathematical operations happening inside each layer amplify dramatically as the neurons and connections are increased. Figure 2.1 shows a simple neural network with three hidden layers, each of them containing seven neurons. In this example (Figure 2.1), between the layers, neurons are fully connected to the neurons of the previous layer. In the end, after a reasonable number of iterations, weights and biases in each neuron get updated to map the three outputs from the four inputs.

Figure 2.2 focuses on the operations inside one of the neurons in hidden layers. This operation can be divided into two steps of computation. First, z is calculated using the weights ($\mathbf{W}$), bias ($\mathbf{b}$), and inputs ($\mathbf{x}$). Second, the activation function $\sigma(z)$ is computed using z. In this example figure (Figure 2.2), a sigmoid activation function is chosen to demonstrate the functionality of a neuron. Here, we could say that the output of a neuron is a function of a function.

The sigmoid activation function (shown in Figure 2.2) has the ability to map any predicted value between 0 and 1. This output can be used to estimate the probability, where a threshold or tipping point (e.g., 0.5) is used

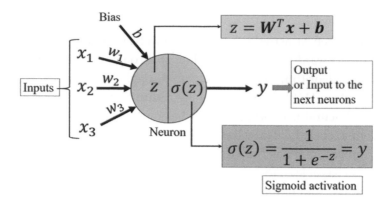

FIGURE 2.2 Computational steps inside a neuron of the hidden layer. Here, $\sigma(z)$ is the sigmoid activation, x_1, x_2, x_3 are inputs to the neuron, w_1, w_2, w_3 are the weights, and b is the bias to the input [10]. (From Tariq M. Arif, Introduction to Deep Learning for Engineers Using Python and Google Cloud Platform, 2020, Chap 3, Page 19, Springer Nature, with permission from Springer Nature.)

for binary classification problems. For example, if *output* ≥ 0.5, class = 1, and if *output* < 0.5, class = 0. There are many other types of activation functions available for an artificial neural network. It is one of the critical selection parameters that dictate training performance.

The use of sigmoid activation in a deep neural network is minimal, and most of the time, non-linear activations such as tanh, ReLU, and Softmax are used. It is important to note that different types of activations can exist in the neurons of the hidden and output layer. Only the neurons of the input layer don't require activation functions. The derivatives of activation functions also play an essential role as they are used in the backpropagation (Section 2.6) error calculation during gradient descent. A short description of typical activation functions and their derivatives is given in the following sections for reference.

2.2.1 Sigmoid Activation

The sigmoid activation and its derivative are defined by equations 2.1 and 2.2, respectively.

$$\sigma(z)=\frac{1}{1+e^{-z}} \tag{2.1}$$

and

$$\sigma'(z)=\sigma(z)\big(1-\sigma(z)\big) \tag{2.2}$$

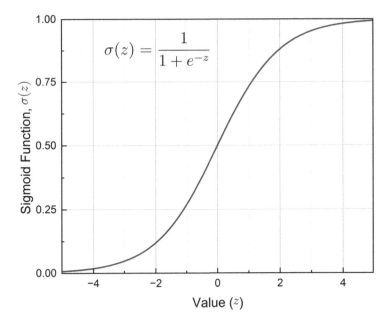

FIGURE 2.3　Plot of Sigmoid activation function between −5 and +5.

This function is also known as the logistic regression function and can be used to determine the probability between 0 and 1. Sometimes, the sigmoid function exists only in the output layer of a neural network for doing the binary classifications. A plot of sigmoid function in the range from −5 to +5 is given in Figure 2.3.

2.2.2　Hyperbolic Tangent Activation

Hyperbolic tangent, also known as tanh function, and its derivative are defined by equations 2.3 and 2.4, respectively.

$$\sigma(z) = \frac{e^z - e^{-z}}{e^z + e^{-z}} \tag{2.3}$$

and

$$\sigma'(z) = \left(1 - \sigma(z)^2\right) \tag{2.4}$$

A hyperbolic tangent function performs better than a sigmoid function when the output is a large negative number. This function can also map any number between −1 and +1. A plot of the hyperbolic tangent function in the range from −5 to +5 is given in Figure 2.4.

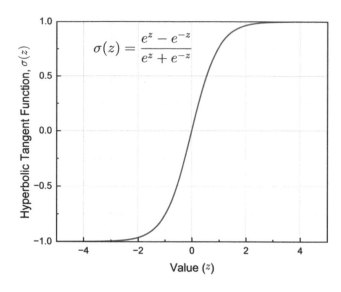

FIGURE 2.4   Plot of hyperbolic tangent activation function between −5 and +5.

2.2.3 Rectified Linear Units (ReLU) Activation

The Rectified Linear Units (ReLU) activation and its derivatives are defined by equations 2.5 and 2.6, respectively.

$$\sigma(z)=\begin{cases} 0 \text{ for } z\le 0 \\ z \text{ for } z>0 \end{cases} \tag{2.5}$$

and

$$\sigma'(z)=\begin{cases} 0 \text{ for } z\le 0 \\ 1 \text{ for } z>0 \end{cases} \tag{2.6}$$

The ReLu function updates parameters faster as its gradient calculation is more straightforward than other activations. It is also used to mitigate the vanishing gradient problem during the backpropagation of the training process. A plot of the ReLU function in the range between −1 and +1 is given in Figure 2.5.

2.2.4 Leaky Rectified Linear Unit (Leaky ReLU) Activation

The Leaky Rectified Linear Unit (Leaky ReLU) is a type of improved ReLU activation that doesn't have 0 slopes for negative values. The regular ReLU activation function may only output zeros during training, which is also known as the dying ReLU problem. The Leaky ReLU solves this problem

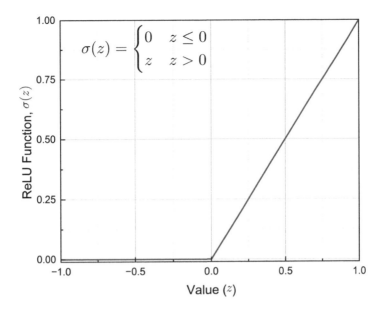

$$\sigma(z) = \begin{cases} 0 & z \leq 0 \\ z & z > 0 \end{cases}$$

FIGURE 2.5 Plot of ReLU activation function between −1 and +1.

since it doesn't have a slope of zero. Leaky ReLU and its derivatives can be defined by equations 2.7 and 2.8, respectively.

$$\sigma(z) = \begin{cases} az \text{ for } z \leq 0 \\ z \text{ for } z > 0 \end{cases} \tag{2.7}$$

and

$$\sigma'(z) = \begin{cases} a \text{ for } z \leq 0 \\ 1 \text{ for } z > 0 \end{cases} \tag{2.8}$$

Here, a in the equations represents a small number (e.g., 0.1). A plot of the Leaky ReLU function in the range between −1 and +1 is given in Figure 2.6.

2.2.5 Exponential Linear Units (ELU) Activation

The Exponential Linear Units (ELU) and its derivatives can be defined by equations 2.9 and 2.10, respectively.

$$\sigma(z) = \begin{cases} a(e^z - 1) \text{ for } z \leq 0 \\ z \text{ for } z > 0 \end{cases} \tag{2.9}$$

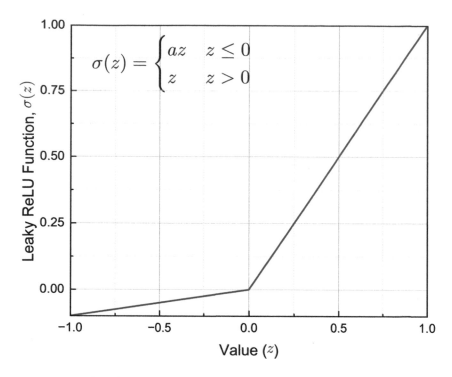

FIGURE 2.6　Plot of Leaky ReLU activation function between −1 and +1.

and

$$\sigma'(z)=\begin{cases}\sigma(z)+a \text{ for } z\leq0\\ \quad 1 \text{ for } z>0\end{cases} \qquad (2.10)$$

Here, a in the equations represents a small number (e.g., 0.5). A plot of the ELU function in the range from −5 to +5 is given in Figure 2.7. ELU activation function converges faster in learning compared to other functions, and it pushes the mean of the activations closer to zero.

2.2.6 SoftPlus Activation

The Soft Plus activation function and its derivative are defined by equations 2.11 and 2.12, respectively.

$$\sigma(z)=\ln(1+e^x) \qquad (2.11)$$

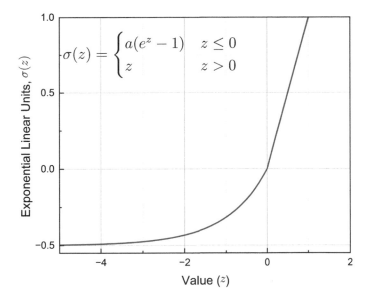

FIGURE 2.7 Plot of ELU activation function between −5 and +2.

and

$$\sigma'(z) = \frac{1}{1+e^{-x}} \qquad (2.12)$$

The Softplus function is smoother than the ReLU function, and its derivative becomes a sigmoid function. But due to exponential operation, it is not as fast as ReLU activation. A plot of Softplus activation in the range from −5 to +2 is given in Figure 2.8.

Finding out the appropriate activation function for a model is a challenge when it has very small gradients during the backpropagation steps. This phenomenon is also known as diminishing gradients. The selection of an activation function that is differentiable in a broad range is very critical for gradient-based optimization and for a successful training process. Besides the activation functions shown here (Sections 2.2.1–2.2.6), many other activation functions are continuously being explored and added in the field of machine learning or deep learning. A few examples are Parametric ReLU, Randomized ReLU, Concatenated ReLU, Bounded ReLU, Parametric Tanh Linear Unit (PTELU), Elastic ReLU (EReLU), Scaled ELU (SELU), Parametric Rectified Exponential Unit (PREU), etc. [11–16]. An extensive survey of newly developed activation functions and their performance reviews are available at [17].

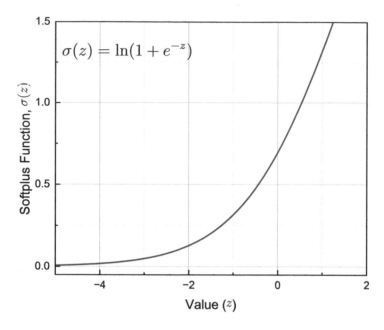

FIGURE 2.8   Plot of Softplus activation function between −5 and +2.

2.3 INTRODUCING NONLINEARITY USING ACTIVATION FUNCTIONS

Deep learning models (artificial networks with many hidden layers) require nonlinear activation functions inside the neurons to train or learn from complex datasets. The activation function examples shown in Section 2.2 are nonlinear and widely used in deep learning training. Linear activation function (e.g., $\sigma(z)=z$) has very few use cases except in some regression problems in machine learning. The reason is if a linear activation function moves forward to the next layer's neuron, it produces another linear function, and regardless of the number of hidden layers used, the final output layer will be a linear function of the first layer. In some regression problems, linear activation can be used only in the final layer, while the hidden layers contain some form of nonlinear activations (e.g., ReLU, ELU, etc.). Also, the linear activation function is not suitable for updating weights during backpropagation calculations, as the derivatives of the cost function always remain constant with respect to the input. For these reasons, nonlinear activation functions are an integral part of deep learning, where networks have to learn complex tasks using backpropagation. Depending on the scenarios, different nonlinear activations can be applied. For example, ReLU activation is widely used in the hidden layers of Convolutional

Neural Networks, softmax is used in the output layer of multiclass classification problems, and sigmoid activation is used in the output layer of a network that determines probabilities.

2.4 INITIALIZATION AND OPTIMIZATION

2.4.1 Weight Initialization

Weight initialization is a key aspect of deep learning modeling. The initial set of weights in all the neurons of the deep learning network dictates how well the learning procedure would be for the backpropagation algorithm. Generally, biases of the network are initialized with zeros, and weights are initialized with random numbers. If zero weights are chosen instead of a random number, during backpropagation, the derivatives with respect to the loss function will remain the same for all weights, and iterations won't have any effect in updating the weights. On the other hand, if the same weights are used for all the neurons, weights will update symmetrically, and the network won't be able to map inputs to outputs. Therefore initial weights are always very sensitive to network performance, and a poor choice of initial weights won't be able to learn anything significant from the training.

The most common initialization technique is to use random initial weights that are not too large or too small. This is very critical because, with a high weight value, the possibility of an exploding gradient problem gets very high, where weights update to infinity due to overshoot. And with a very small weight, gradients get much smaller during backpropagation, and the possibility of the vanishing gradient problem increases. There are various methods available that can be used for weight initialization, and a wide variety of methods with minor variations are continuously being explored for suitable weight initialization approaches. A few examples are LeCun initialization [18], initialization with truncated normal distribution [19], Xavier Glorot Initialization [20], Kaiming He initialization [11], Modified Nguyen–Widrow initialization [21], etc. All the standard deep learning frameworks, such as TensorFlow, PyTorch, and Keras, provide various built-in weight initialization functions to initialize neuron weights using random small numbers within a reasonable range.

2.4.2 Weight Regularization

Weight regularization approach can address the problem of overfitting during the training process. It introduces additional layer parameters to the network for generalizing the function. If the training process becomes too complex and starts to generate large weights, the regularization approach adds a penalty term to the loss function. Typically, the regularization parameter is represented by λ, which is a small number, and a cost function can be used after regularization, as shown in equation 2.13.

$$\text{Cost} = \text{Loss Function} + \frac{\lambda}{2m} \sum_{i=1}^{n} \left\| w^{[i]} \right\|^2 \qquad (2.13)$$

where λ = regularization parameter, m = number of inputs, n = number of layers, $w^{[i]}$ = weight matrix for i-th layer. When the augmented error is minimized using a small regularization term λ, complex or large weights are reduced. The regularization shown in equation 2.13 is known as L2 regularization (ridge regression or Tikhonov regularization) since it penalizes the sum of square values of weights. Generally, L2 regularization is used in most cases, but in some feature selection cases, L1 regularization is used where the sum of absolute values of weights is used, as shown in equation 2.14.

$$\text{Cost} = \text{Loss Function} + \frac{\lambda}{2m} \sum_{i=1}^{n} \left\| w^{[i]} \right\| \qquad (2.14)$$

The regularization parameter, λ is known as a hyperparameter and needs to be fine-tuned for better training.

2.4.2.1 Weight Decay

Weight decay is another simple regularization technique that directly uses a penalty co-efficient (typically denoted by λ) for each layer to reduce the weights and prevent overfitting. It is a form of L2 regularization as it can be derived from the gradient of the L2 norm of the weights in the gradient descent setting [22]. In some contexts, using a single weight decay coefficient can be cost-effective since there will be fewer parameters for hyperparameter tuning.

2.4.2.2 Dropout

Dropout is a form of powerful regularization technique that can address the overfitting problem during the training process. It randomly switches off a pre-defined percentage of neurons from each layer in each iteration. All the connections of those switched-off neurons become disabled, and the updated network becomes a diminished version of the original neural network. This process of dropping off random neurons is proven to be helpful for reducing overfitting and can produce a wide distribution of weights.

2.4.3 Optimizer

During the training process, the optimizer utilizes an algorithm to search weights or biases that minimize the error or the loss function. There are various types of optimizers available for training, and choosing the right kind of optimizer depends on the types of tasks that the neural network tries to learn. The most common type of optimizer is gradient descent which uses the derivatives of the loss function to find minimum errors. Details explanation of the gradient descent algorithm is given in Section 2.5.1 of this chapter. The gradient descent algorithm has some variations, such as stochastic gradient descent, batch gradient descent, and mini-batch gradient descent, that are also widely used by researchers and data scientists.

In deep learning training, mini-batch optimizers are used to calculate the loss function for a small batch instead of the entire dataset. Some mini-batch optimizers use adaptive learning rates for individual network connections to avoid sign reversal or decreased learning rates (e.g., Adagrad, Adadelta, RMSProp). Other variations of mini-batch optimizers are the Nesterov Accelerated Gradient (NAG) and Adaptive moment optimizer (e.g., Adam), which can calculate adaptive learning rates for each parameter in an efficient way. Each of the optimizers has its advantages and drawbacks. Although the gradient descent optimization algorithm uses first-order derivatives, some studies successfully implemented second-order derivatives for updating weights during training [23, 24]. Currently, all the popular deep learning frameworks provide several built-in optimizers for the users, and a wide range of new optimizers are continuously being explored by researchers.

2.4.4 Batch Normalization

Batch normalization is an algorithm that normalizes the activations of hidden layers to make the training process more effective and faster. In the deep learning network, inputs are normalized, but after multiple layers, they no longer remain normalized due to the computations in each neuron, and the learning process of the network becomes very slow. To overcome this issue, the batch normalization approach was introduced by Sergey Ioffe and Christia Szegedy in 2015 [25]. It calculates the mean (μ) and variance (σ^2) of the activation values of a hidden layer, and then normalizes those using equation 2.17. Equations 2.15 and 2.16 show the formula for calculating mean and variance, respectively. After the normalization, layers will have activation values with 0 mean and unit standard deviation. Then the layer output is scaled and shifted (for all batches) by using equation 2.18, which utilizes two learnable parameters, γ and β. These learnable parameters help to calibrate values for different batches, where γ finds a mean and β finds a variance, applicable to all batches. The batch normalization algorithm also keeps track of the exponential moving average of the mean and variance and saves the final or most recent value for model inference or testing.

$$\mu = \frac{1}{m} \sum_{i=1}^{m} z_i \qquad (2.15)$$

$$\sigma^2 = \frac{1}{m} \sum_{i=1}^{m} (z_i - \mu)^2 \qquad (2.16)$$

$$\hat{z}_i = \frac{z_i - \mu}{\sqrt{\sigma^2 + \epsilon}} \qquad (2.17)$$

$$\tilde{z}_i = \gamma \hat{z}_i + \beta \qquad (2.18)$$

where μ = mean for a batch, m = batch size, σ^2 = variance for a batch, ϵ = a small number, γ and β = learnable parameters, and $\tilde{z}_i$ = layer output.

During the model testing, batch normalization needs to be used differently as the model requires checking the data one by one instead of batches. Therefore, the algorithm estimates another mean and variance that are final values of exponentially weighted averages from training batches. Using the estimated mean and variance, normalized $\hat{z}_i$ and transformed $\tilde{z}_i$ are calculated from equations 2.17 and 2.18.

2.5 MINIMIZING THE LOSS FUNCTION

The loss function is the quantity that is minimized during model training [5]. It is also known as the objective function or error function. A neural network may have multiple loss functions based on the number of outputs. A classification model should have a cross-entropy loss or a log loss of 0. Generally, for a two-class classification problem, binary cross-entropy and for multiclass classification problems, categorical cross-entropy is used. The learning process of a neural network is basically finding out weights and biases to minimize the loss function.

Typically, the loss function is also called the cost function if the error is calculated for the entire training set or a batch. The standard binary cross-entropy loss function can be defined by equation 2.19 [12],

$$J = -\frac{1}{M}\sum_{m=1}^{M}\left[y_m \times \log\left(h_\theta\left(x_m\right)\right) + \left(1 - y_m\right) \times \log\left(1 - h_\theta\left(x_m\right)\right)\right] \qquad (2.19)$$

Where M = number of training examples, y_m = target label for training example m, x_m = input for training example m, h_θ = model with neural network weights θ. For categorical targets, if $\hat{y}_1 \ldots \ldots \ldots \hat{y}_m$ are the probabilities of the "m" classes, and the r-th class is the ground-truth class, then the loss function for a single instance is defined by equation 2.20 [13],

$$J = -\log\left(\hat{y}_r\right) \qquad (2.20)$$

The goal of any neural network is to minimize this equation (Eq. 2.20). The minimization process is done by updating weights using an optimization function or optimizer. An important iterative algorithm known as backpropagation is used to apply this optimization, and in this process, the loss function dictates how well the network is learning. The selection of a suitable loss function depends on the computational scenario, and they typically differ in their simulation speed and convergence ability.

2.5.1 Gradient Descent Algorithm

The gradient descent is an iterative first-order optimization algorithm that helps the neural network to minimize the cost function, J. In the case of linear regression, we can use derivatives to find a minimum of convex functions. But in the artificial neural network, we always deal with a non-convex function, and therefore gradient descent algorithm can end up finding the local minima instead of global minima.

Figure 2.9 shows how the gradient descent can end up in different minima (solutions) based on the starting point. This example is for only one weight parameter, ω. For a 3D surface plot where the cost function J is a function of two parameters (ω and b) and forms a non-convex shape, the gradient descent algorithm may also converge to a local minima instead of a global one as shown in Figure 2.10. Here, the height of the surface shows the value of the cost function J for respective weight and bias.

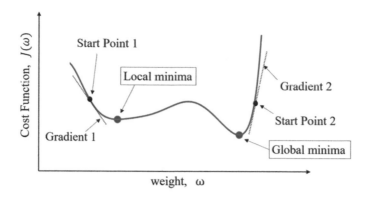

FIGURE 2.9   If the initial starting point is Start Point 1, the gradient descent algorithm will converge to a local minima. On the other hand, if Start Point 2 is used, the algorithm will converge to the global minima [10]. (From Tariq M. Arif, Introduction to Deep Learning for Engineers Using Python and Google Cloud Platform, 2020, Chap 3, Page 25, Springer Nature, with permission from Springer Nature.)

In most machine learning optimization tasks, the cost function is a higher-dimensional function due to the existence of many weights and biases. This type of higher-dimensional plot is impossible to visualize. However, the gradient descent algorithm can simultaneously be performed for all values of weights and biases. If we have n neurons in a hidden layer, all the weights will update through equation 2.21 [14]. Here α is the learning rate, which tells the algorithm how big or small the step size would be while

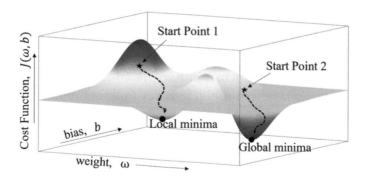

FIGURE 2.10   If the Cost function, J is a function of two parameters (weight and bias), the gradient descent algorithm will search for a minima on the surface. In this example plot, Start Point 1 will converge to a local minima, and Start Point 2 will converge to a global minima [10]. (From Tariq M. Arif, Introduction to Deep Learning for Engineers Using Python and Google Cloud Platform, 2020, Chap 3, Page 26, Springer Nature, with permission from Springer Nature.)

moving in the direction of downhill steep. The negative gradients push the algorithm to move toward the downhill direction.

$$\omega_1 = \omega_1 - \alpha \frac{\partial}{\partial \omega_1} J(\omega, b)$$

$$\omega_2 = \omega_2 - \alpha \frac{\partial}{\partial \omega_2} J(\omega, b)$$

$$\omega_3 = \omega_3 - \alpha \frac{\partial}{\partial \omega_3} J(\omega, b)$$

$$\cdot$$
$$\cdot$$ (2.21)
$$\cdot$$
$$\cdot$$

$$\omega_n = \omega_n - \alpha \frac{\partial}{\partial \omega_n} J(\omega, b)$$

The bias parameters for a hidden layer can be updated using equation 2.22.

$$b = b - \alpha \frac{\partial}{\partial b} J(\omega, b) \qquad (2.22)$$

Equations 2.21 and 2.22 shows the calculation for one layer only. Therefore, this computational process becomes very complex and expensive in the case of deep learning when we have many hidden layers. Here, the learning rate, α is one of the critical hyper-parameters for model training, and it needs to be tuned carefully. If the learning rate is too low, the gradient descent algorithm will become computationally expensive and may not find a global solution. On the other hand, if the learning rate is relatively big, it may overshoot the minima and fail to converge.

One way to use the learning rate effectively is to reduce its value as the training progresses. This process can be achieved by using an adaptive learning rate [15]. The adaptive learning rate can be reduced or adjusted using a pre-defined schedule, such as time-based decay, step decay, and exponential decay [16]. Many algorithms, such as Adam, SGD, AdaGrad, and RMSProp, use the adaptive learning rate. The PyTorch "torch.optim" package also has built-in functions that allow users to pass arguments in different optimizers for implementing the adaptive learning algorithm [17].

2.6 FORWARD AND BACKPROPAGATION

Forward and backpropagation are the key operations of deep learning where the model actually learns from a given dataset or input-output pattern. In forward propagation, input signals to the network pass through the layers and compute the activations of the neurons until the output layer is reached. These activations are calculated in neurons by multiplying the input values with their corresponding weights and adding the bias, then passing this value through an activation function to find the neuron's output. The outputs from each layer of neurons serve as the inputs for the next layer of neurons up to the final output layer. The outputs or predictions from the network are then compared to desired or target outputs using a loss function such as mean squared error or cross-entropy loss.

In backpropagation, the model computes the gradients of the loss function with respect to the weights and biases of the neural network by propagating backward through the network. This operation is done by employing the chain rule of differentiation, which uses the partial derivatives of composite functions layer after layer. The gradients then update weights and biases to minimize the loss function. This update policy in backpropagation is done by using any suitable optimization algorithm, such as gradient descent, stochastic gradient descent, RMSProp, Adam, etc.

2.7 HYPERPARAMETERS

Hyperparameters are model parameters that are not learned by the training process, but they can dictate how well or poorly the model is going to learn. For example, during the training process, the algorithm is capable of updating weights and biases to minimize the loss function, but it doesn't have controls over other pre-defined parameters set by the user, such as the number of hidden layers or neurons, types of activation functions, etc. These parameters that can directly influence the model's behavior and performance but can't be updated through training are known as hyperparameters.

2.7.1 Fine-Tuning Hyperparameters

There is no definitive rule or procedure for fine-tuning hyperparameters, and typically, they are selected through various experimentation and trial-and-error. Since these parameters are not learned from the data, the programmer's intuition and prior experience play a significant role when fine-tuning the hyperparameters. Also, it depends on the specific problems and data types. For example, the hyperparameter tuning for computer vision problems may not work properly with natural language processing problems.

For the fine-tuning process, it is recommended to observe the effect of different hyperparameters on the model's performance. A model may not be sensitive to a specific hyperparameter but can have a significant impact on any change to other parameters. However, sometimes, it is wise to use a standard or default value of hyperparameter if it doesn't have any apparent significance. For example, in deep learning number of layers can be selected arbitrarily. It is well-established that using more hidden layers and neurons is suitable for learning very complex representations from a dataset, but it can also be very challenging and computationally expensive. Therefore selecting an appropriate number of hidden layers can be tricky, and proper judgment or intuition is necessary for using available resources.

The learning rate hyperparameter can be tuned to determine the step size during iterations. A high learning rate may help the model to converge quickly, but there is a risk of overshooting an optimum result. On the other hand, a low learning rate can make the training process very slow and can converge into a local solution. The batch size used in training is another hyperparameter that determines the number of training samples going to the networks in each iteration and is highly sensitive to the memory and computational power of the workstation. A smaller batch size is suitable for convergence but can make the model unstable. The large batch size can work better in parallel processing but is slow in training and may find a suboptimal solution to the problem.

Other key hyperparameters include the regularization techniques used, drop-out rates, parameters for batch normalization, activation functions, optimization algorithms, etc. Some recent studies used advanced hyper-parameter search methods such as evolutionary algorithms and Bayesian optimizations [26–30]. So overall, in deep learning, hyperparameters should be selected and fine-tuned based on the problem specifications and dataset properties. If enough computation power is available, hyperparameters can also be searched using random search and grid search methods.

2.7.2 Batch, Iteration, and Epoch

Batch, iteration, and epoch numbers are hyperparameters that can influence deep learning performance, and these numbers should be selected carefully considering the dataset type and computational capacity of the workstation.

The batch is the subset of the training dataset that is fed to the network in one go instead of the entire dataset. If the entire dataset is fed to the network, the deep learning model becomes computationally expensive, and generally, it is even impossible due to memory constraints. Therefore deep learning algorithm uses smaller subsets or "batches". For example, in a dataset with 50,000 training samples, if a batch size of 500 is used, the model will intake 500 samples at a time to make one prediction. A key benefit of using batches is that they allow the model to update its weights and biases more frequently, which can accelerate the learning and improve stability.

An iteration in deep learning refers to updating the model's parameter once. During the training process, the model takes one batch at a time from the dataset and makes predictions, computes errors using the loss function, and then updates weights and biases using a gradient-based optimization algorithm. This entire process is an iteration. Therefore the iteration number is dependent on both batch size and the total number of samples. For example, in a dataset with 50,000 training samples, if a batch size of 500 is used, the model will need 50,000/500, that is, 100 iterations, to go through the entire dataset once.

Epoch is another key hyperparameter in deep learning that refers to one complete pass through the entire dataset. After an epoch, the model sees all the samples from the training dataset and updates its weights and biases. For example, in a dataset with 50,000 training samples, if a batch size of 500 is used, after 100 iterations, the model goes through the complete dataset, and therefore, one epoch will be in 100 iterations. Therefore, if the model is trained for ten epochs, the entire training dataset is processed through the network ten times. Epoch numbers should be selected carefully, as too many or too few epochs can cause the model to overfit or underfit, respectively.

2.7.3 Cross-Validation

Cross-validation is a commonly used approach for assessing the generalization and accomplishment of the model. It is widely used in deep learning and in any other predictive modeling when a fixed or limited amount of samples are available. The most common form of cross-validation is k-fold cross-validation which divides a dataset randomly into multiple subsets or "folds". For example, in k-fold cross-validation, if $k = 10$, the dataset would be shuffled and divided into ten subsets with an equal number of samples. The model will then be trained and tested 10 times ($k = 10$), and each time, one of the subsets will be left out during the training process, and after training, that left-out data group will be used for testing or validation. In deep learning, cross-validation is trickier to use as it requires more computational resources than machine learning or other predictive modeling approaches. However, the way the cross-validation algorithm implements variability and randomness is helpful for the learning process.

If computational resources are available, Cross-validation can be a very helpful tool for hyperparameter tuning as it tries to ensure that the model is not overfitting during the training process. Typically, after cross-validation, the model demonstrates poor performance with new or unseen data. However, it allows the model to perform robustly after averaging the performance over multiple train-test splits.

2.8 DEEP TRANSFER LEARNING

Transfer learning is a method of applying the knowledge of a pre-trained network to another model when we have insufficient data and computing resources to train a new model from scratch. Using this method, knowledge learned from one type of data can be applied to totally different types of data. In recent years, deep convolutional networks have shown tremendous success in image recognition and classification tasks using transfer learning methods [31, 32]. One of the key challenges to training a deep learning model from the beginning is that it requires a vast amount of labeled dataset, which is not common in many practical scenarios. Generally, a model can make good predictions if it is trained on a big dataset. There are many deep learning models available that are developed by training on big datasets, such as ImageNet, MNIST, MS COCO, Caltech datasets, Pascal VOC, CIFAR10, and so on. The performance of a deep learning model generally increases if it is trained on a big dataset. For example, the popular ImageNet dataset contains 14,197,122 images, and the Tina Image contains 79,302,017 images [33, 34]. We can import deep learning models that are trained on some established and properly labeled dataset. These models can be imported and customized a little to match the requirements (e.g., input and output features) of specific training tasks.

2.8.1 Types of Transfer Learning

The relationship between traditional machine learning and transfer learning can be categorized into three different ways, according to Pan et al. [35]: inductive, transductive, and unsupervised learning. The inductive transfer learning method can be built by infusing similar instances from different learning tasks, transductive transfer learning can be used when the source and target tasks are the same, and the unsupervised transfer learning does unsupervised learning tasks (e.g., clustering, dimensionality reduction). Pan et al. [35] also sub-categorized transfer learning approaches based on instance, feature-representation, parameter, and relational knowledge transfers. Transfer learning often has a variety of practices and can also be used for initialization or fine-tuning purposes.

2.8.2 Pre-Trained Networks

If we want to use a dataset for supervised learning, we will need to label or annotate data for training. Annotating a large volume of data, which is an integral part of deep learning, would be extremely time-consuming. Fortunately, there is an easy way to avoid this by implementing knowledge from a pre-trained model architecture that has already been trained on a different dataset. There are many pre-trained models available that we can use effectively, and the amount of effort required for this process is also relatively insignificant. Some of the widely used pre-trained networks are ResNet, GoogleLeNet, VGG, Inception, DenseNet, VGG, EfficientNet, etc [36]. Many other ready-to-use pre-trained models are available now, and as the field of deep learning is emerging, new models are continuously being tested and added to this list.

One of the advantages of using pre-trained networks is that the architectures have already been trained and tested using a large dataset (e.g., ImageNet). We can just use these networks partially or wholly in the transfer learning process. For partial uses of a model, only the last few layers are regulated to train it on a new dataset, but the core parts of the network are kept unchanged. On the other hand, we can also utilize the whole architecture without parameter values, initialize all the weights randomly, and then train the model using a new dataset. These simple techniques can significantly boost the performance of a deep learning model, and recently, these types of transfer learning practices have becoming well-accepted in computer vision applications [37–39]. The PyTroch package "torchvision" has many popular model architectures that we can use for deep transfer learning [40].

2.8.3 Feature Extraction and Data Augmentation

Deep learning architectures learn features layer by layer. For example, when a convolutional network learns from images, it tends to learn patterns, textures, edges, and brightness in the first few layers. These features from images are used for processing many different types of natural images, and they can be reused. Typically the last few layers of a deep learning network are very specific to the current task. So, for a classification problem, if we utilize a pre-train model for transfer learning without using its last layer, we will easily get the hidden states of the trained network to extract some standard features. For a more rigorous training process, we can reconfigure some of the layers of the model (especially the last few) before retraining it on the new data. This step will fine-tune the whole model, but the successful implementation of this approach depends on the dataset and the prediction task we are trying to accomplish.

If we have a relatively less amount of data for deep learning, we can use the data augmentation technique to improve model performance. Augmentation will manipulate the training images in different ways, such as flipping, rotating, shearing, cropping, shifting RGB channels, and so on. As a result, we will get various unique and relevant images from a single image. It will increase the amount of training data representation of our model. Recently, different data augmentation techniques have been explored by researchers to improve the validation accuracy of a model. We will show a practical implementation of pre-trained weights, fine-tuning, and data augmentation in the case studies presented in this book.

2.8.4 Model Evaluation

During training, we will initially need to split our annotated data sets into training and test sets. The training data (which can be subdivided into training and validation sets) will be used to learn the model parameters, and test data will estimate the accuracy of the learned model. Typically, a large test set will do a good estimation with low variance. There are different types of metrics available that are used in model evaluation, such as confusion matrix, accuracy, F1 score, and so on.

To evaluate the model, we can initially check classification accuracy, especially when we have an almost equal number of samples for different classes. It is just the ratio of correct predictions to the total number of predictions. The confusion matrix can be used to demonstrate the quality of output results shown in a matrix, where higher diagonal values indicate many correct results. A confusion matrix can be constructed by finding true positive (model predicted positive, which is a true result), false positive (model predicted positive, which is a false result), true negative (model predicted negative, which is a true result), and false negative (model predicted negative, which is a false result). From the values of the matrix, we can calculate precision, recall, and weighted F1 scores to understand the relevance and model performance. Evaluation metrics should be selected based on the task performed by a model. It is always better to check multiple metrics to evaluate a model since a model may perform differently in different matrics. The case studies presented in this book have a significant amount of training data. Therefore, for a simpler evaluation, we showed only the training and validation losses or accuracies in the case studies.

REFERENCES

1. Abiodun, O. I., Jantan, A., Omolara, A. E., Dada, K. V., Mohamed, N. A., and Arshad, H., 2018, "State-of-the-Art in Artificial Neural Network Applications: A Survey," Heliyon, 4(11), p. e00938.
2. Mehdy, M. M., Ng, P. Y., Shair, E. F., Saleh, N. I. M., and Gomes, C., 2017, "Artificial Neural Networks in Image Processing for Early Detection of Breast Cancer," Computational and Mathematical Methods in Medicine, 2017, p. 2610628.
3. Araque, O., Corcuera-Platas, I., Sánchez-Rada, J. F., and Iglesias, C. A., 2017, "Enhancing Deep Learning Sentiment Analysis with Ensemble Techniques in Social Applications," Expert Systems with Applications, 77, pp. 236–246.
4. Zhou, X., Gong, W., Fu, W., and Du, F., 2017, "Application of deep learning in object detection," 2017 IEEE/ACIS 16th International Conference on Computer and Information Science (ICIS), IEEE, pp. 631–634.
5. Pichler, M., and Hartig, F., 2023, "Machine Learning and Deep Learning—A Review for Ecologists," Methods in Ecology and Evolution, 14(4), pp. 994–1016.
6. Li, L., Zhang, S., and Wang, B., 2021, "Plant Disease Detection and Classification by Deep Learning-A Review," IEEE Access, 9, pp. 56683–56698.
7. Lenail, A., 2019, "NN-SVG," https://github.com/alexlenail/NN-SVG.
8. Goodfellow, I., Bengio, Y., and Courville, A., 2016, Deep Learning, MIT Press.
9. Alex, 2020, "Feedforward Neural Networks and Multilayer Perceptrons," https://boostedml.com/2020/04/feedforward-neural-networks-and-multilayer-perceptrons.html.
10. Arif, T. M., 2020, "Basic Artificial Neural Network and Architectures," Introduction to Deep Learning for Engineers: Using Python and Google Cloud Platform, Springer International Publishing, Cham, pp. 17–27.
11. He, K., Zhang, X., Ren, S., and Sun, J., 2015, "Delving deep into rectifiers: surpassing human-level performance on ImageNet classification," IEEE International Conference on Computer Vision (ICCV 2015), IEEE, p. 1502.
12. Shang, W., Sohn, K., Almeida, D., and Lee, H., 2016, "Understanding and Improving Convolutional Neural Networks via Concatenated Rectified Linear Units," Proceedings of International Conference on Machine Learning, PMLR, pp. 2217–2225.
13. Duggal, R., and Gupta, A., 2017, "P-TELU: Parametric Tan Hyperbolic Linear Unit Activation for Deep Neural Networks," Proceedings of the IEEE International Conference on Computer Vision Workshops, pp. 974–978.

14. Liew, S. S., Khalil-Hani, M., and Bakhteri, R., 2016, "Bounded Activation Functions for Enhanced Training Stability of Deep Neural Networks on Visual Pattern Recognition Problems," Neurocomputing, 216, pp. 718–734.

15. Jiang, X., Pang, Y., Li, X., Pan, J., and Xie, Y., 2018, "Deep Neural Networks with Elastic Rectified Linear Units for Object Recognition," Neurocomputing, 275, pp. 1132–1139.

16. Ying, Y., Su, J., Shan, P., Miao, L., Wang, X., and Peng, S., 2019, "Rectified Exponential Units for Convolutional Neural Networks," IEEE Access, 7, pp. 101633–101640.

17. Dubey, S. R., Singh, S. K., and Chaudhuri, B. B., 2022, "Activation Functions in Deep Learning: A Comprehensive Survey and Benchmark," Neurocomputing, 503, pp. 92–108.

18. Bagheri, R., 2020, "Weight Initialization in Deep Neural Networks," https://towardsdatascience.com/weight-initialization-in-deep-neural-networks-268a306540c0.

19. Rubin, O., 2023, "Conversations with GPT-4: Weight Initialization with the Truncated Normal Distribution," https://medium.com/@ohadrubin/conversations-with-gpt-4-weight-initialization-with-the-truncated-normal-distribution-78a9f71bc478.

20. Hlav, E., 2022, "Xavier Glorot Initialization in Neural Networks—Math Proof," https://towardsdatascience.com/xavier-glorot-initialization-in-neural-networks-math-proof-4682bf5c6ec3.

21. Mittal, A., Singh, A. P., and Chandra, P., "A Modification to the Nguyen–Widrow Weight Initialization Method," Intelligent Systems, Technologies and Applications, S. M. Thampi, L. Trajkovic, S. Mitra, P. Nagabhushan, J. Mukhopadhyay, J. M. Corchado, S. Berretti, and D. Mishra, eds., Springer, Singapore, pp. 141–153.

22. Zhang, G., Wang, C., Xu, B., and Grosse, R., 2019, "Three Mechanisms of Weight Decay Regularization." International Conference on Learning Representations (ICLR) (Poster), New Orleans, LA.

23. Anil, R., Gupta, V., Koren, T., Regan, K., and Singer, Y., 2021, "Scalable Second Order Optimization for Deep Learning." https://arxiv.org/abs/2002.09018

24. Yao, Z., Gholami, A., Shen, S., Mustafa, M., Keutzer, K., and Mahoney, M., 2021, "ADAHESSIAN: An Adaptive Second Order Optimizer for Machine Learning," Proceedings of the AAAI Conference on Artificial Intelligence, 35(12), pp. 10665–10673.

25. Ioffe, S., and Szegedy, C., 2015, "Batch Normalization: Accelerating Deep Network Training by Reducing Internal Covariate Shift," Proceedings of the 32nd International Conference on Machine Learning, B. Francis, and B. David, eds., PMLR, Proceedings of Machine Learning Research, pp. 448–456.

26. Young, S. R., Rose, D. C., Karnowski, T. P., Lim, S.-H., and Patton, R. M., 2015, "Optimizing Deep Learning Hyper-Parameters through an Evolutionary Algorithm," Proceedings of the Workshop on Machine Learning in High-Performance Computing Environments, Association for Computing Machinery, p. 4.

27. Vincent, A. M., and Jidesh, P., 2023, "An Improved Hyperparameter Optimization Framework for AutoML Systems Using Evolutionary Algorithms," Scientific Reports, 13(1), p. 4737.
28. Tani, L., Rand, D., Veelken, C., and Kadastik, M., 2021, "Evolutionary Algorithms for Hyperparameter Optimization in Machine Learning for Application in High Energy Physics," The European Physical Journal C, 81(2), p. 170.
29. Klein, A., Falkner, S., Bartels, S., Hennig, P., and Hutter, F., 2017, "Fast Bayesian Optimization of Machine Learning Hyperparameters on Large Datasets," Artificial Intelligence and Statistics, PMLR, pp. 528–536.
30. Victoria, A. H., and Maragatham, G., 2021, "Automatic Tuning of Hyperparameters Using Bayesian Optimization," Evolving Systems, 12, pp. 217–223.
31. Shin, H. C., Roth, H. R., Gao, M., Lu, L., Xu, Z., Nogues, I., Yao, J., Mollura, D., and Summers, R. M., 2016, "Deep Convolutional Neural Networks for Computer-Aided Detection: CNN Architectures, Dataset Characteristics and Transfer Learning," IEEE Transactions on Medical Imaging, 35(5), pp. 1285–1298.
32. Marée, R., Geurts, P., and Wehenkel, L., 2016, "Towards Generic Image Classification Using Tree-Based Learning: An Extensive Empirical Study," Pattern Recognition Letters, 74, pp. 17–23.
33. Russakovsky, O., Deng, J., Su, H., Krause, J., Satheesh, S., Ma, S., Huang, Z., Karpathy, A., Khosla, A., Bernstein, M., Berg, A. C., and Fei-Fei, L., 2015, "ImageNet Large Scale Visual Recognition Challenge," International Journal of Computer Vision, 115(3), pp. 211–252.
34. Torralba, A., Fergus, R., and Freeman, W. T., 2008, "80 Million Tiny Images: A Large Data Set for Nonparametric Object and Scene Recognition," IEEE Transactions on Pattern Analysis and Machine Intelligence, 30(11), pp. 1958–1970.
35. Pan, S. J., and Yang, Q., 2010, "A Survey on Transfer Learning," IEEE Transactions on Knowledge and Data Engineering, 22(10), pp. 1345–1359.
36. "Keras Applications," 2023, https://keras.io/api/applications/.
37. Le, Q. V., "Building High-Level Features Using Large Scale Unsupervised Learning," Proceedings 2013 IEEE International Conference on Acoustics, Speech and Signal Processing, IEEE, pp. 8595–8598.
38. Radford, A., Metz, L., and Chintala, S., 2015, "Unsupervised representation learning with deep convolutional generative adversarial networks," https://arxiv.org/abs/1511.06434.
39. Wan, R., Xiong, H., Li, X., Zhu, Z., and Huan, J. 2019, "Towards Making Deep Transfer Learning Never Hurt," 2019 IEEE International Conference on Data Mining (ICDM), IEEE, pp. 578–587.
40. "TORCHVISION.MODELS," 2023, https://pytorch.org/vision/0.8/models.html#.

## CHAPTER 3

Computer Vision Fundamentals

3.1 INTRODUCTION

Computer vision is a part of Artificial Intelligence (AI) that trains computers to "see" and perceive the content of images or videos. It has already accomplished extraordinary milestones in numerous real-world applications and is still considered one of the most emerging technologies. The implementation of computer vision can be found in any field where visual inputs through digital images or videos are available for further analysis. Nowadays, we see the implementation of this technology in the fields of robotics, autonomous vehicles, traffic flow investigations, self-delivery drones, intelligent security systems, Unmanned Aerial Vehicle (UAV) surveying, medical image diagnosis, and much more. The most fundamental operations done in AI-based computer visions can be categorized as image or video classifications [1–5], segmentations [6–10], object detection [11–14], face recognition [15–18], and pattern recognition [19–21]. Overall, computer vision technology assists a computer, robot, or any intelligent system in processing digital images and videos and making knowledgeable outputs or decisions similar to or beyond human-level accuracy.

To apply computer vision, a well-defined image dataset is required. In many cases where structured images are available, computer vision can outperform human performance and can able to detect patterns or features that are challenging to perceive in humans. For example, in healthcare, the AI system was able to diagnose brain tumors better than doctors [22], exhibit better performance in radiomic feature extraction for cancer detection [23], and demonstrate superiority in diagnosing retinal diseases [24] as well as diabetic retinopathy [25]. Other engineering areas where computer vision exceeds human performance include satellite image analysis [26], oil and gas exploration [27, 28], sports review and performance analysis [29], etc. Very recently, CNN models have been used on 3D MRI image data to explore complicated functions of the human brain [30–32]. It should be noted that the performance of computer vision is dependent on the data set on which the model is trained.

In contrast to computer vision, our human brain has a much more complex mechanism of "seeing", and its visual performance is still much superior in constructing invariant representations [33, 34]. Although the way humans see is not properly understood, the computer's method of seeing is relatively straightforward. For instance, a digital image is read as an array of numbers representing the pixel intensities at different points ranging from 0 to 255. If a computer reads the image of a flower, as shown in Figure 3.1,

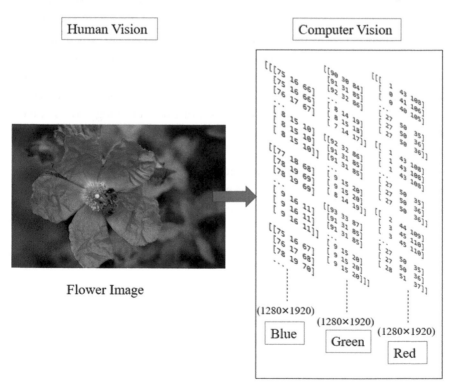

FIGURE 3.1 An image perceived by computers is a number of array layers with different pixel intensities.

and prints it directly in Python, the output will be a big 3D matrix based on image resolution (e.g., 1280 by 1920 by 3 matrix). Here, the image has three different channels (three layers) for RGB colors with 1280 pixels along the height and 1920 pixels along the width.

Over the last few years, we have seen numerous challenging implementations of deep learning for computer vision. Deep learning models are very effective in learning from raw and high-dimensional image data using convolutional neural network (CNN) algorithms. In this chapter, we focus on this CNN algorithm, and a brief overview of its architecture and important features are presented in the following sections.

3.2 CNN ARCHITECTURE

CNN, also known as ConvNets, was initially developed by Yann LeCun for computer vision and image processing [35]. Later on, it was successfully modified by other researchers for improved sentence classification, speech recognition, image segmentation, and image classification tasks [36–39]. For computer-vision-related operations, CNN is the most widely used deep learning method to process grid-structured input data, such as an image with spatial and temporal properties.

A CNN architecture is a multi-layer framework designed to process and transform the input image data to a form that the deep learning model can utilize for training. Generally, after the inputs layer, convolutional and pooling layers are placed at the beginning, and after that, it goes through the fully connected and output layer. The image input in the convolutional layer is typically rearranged in multiple arrays or multi-channeled images. For example, a color image is a combination of three color channels (red, green, and blue), and each of these channels can be presented in a 2D array for the input. Inside the 2D array, the intensities of these color channels are ranged from 0 to 255.

3.2.1 Input Layer

The input layer is the first layer of CNN, where the network receives the pixel values of an image. If the input image is an 8-bit grayscale image, it will have only one shade of black color with pixel intensities ranging from 0 to 255. Here, 0 and 255 correspond to black and white colors, respectively. The grayscale image is often used in computer vision tasks that don't require color information of an image, and training a deep learning model using grayscale images reduces additional complexities. Learning applications where grayscale images are prevalent include document scanning, handwriting recognition, and various medical image analysis.

If the input image is a colorful 8-bit image, it is represented as the combination of three color channels: red, green, and blue (RGB). The combined effect of these three colors produces a broad spectrum of colors using three different channels, and each of these channels also ranges from 0 to 255 (8-bit image). RGB images provide more detailed color information that is useful for object detection or recognition, classification, and segmentation. However, processing color images require more computational resources compared to grayscale image.

3.2.2 Convolutional Layer

Convolutional layers are the primary building block of CNN architecture. These layers implement a set of learnable filters on the training images to extract specific features like colors, edges, or textures. These layers typically slice through image depth, numbers of pixels, or zero-padding around a shape to learn from different sections of three channel inputs. When multiple kernels concatenate with each other, they are called filters which have one more dimension than the kernels. Inside the neural network, each of the kernels will assign a new layer that corresponds to the edges, depths, shapes, or textures of the image.

During the forward propagation process, each filter is convolved across the width and height of the input and computes the dot product between the filter and input to produce a 2D activation map. At this stage, the network tries to learn when they "see" certain features at some spatial position of the input image.

3.2.3 Non-Linearity Layer

To learn sophisticated features from input images and add complexity or depth to the network, non-linearity layers (with nonlinear activations), such as rectified linear units (ReLU) are applied to the output of the convolutional layer. Most real-world data are nonlinear and can't be trained by using linear functions only. Examples of some common nonlinear functions that can be used are Leaky ReLU, sigmoid, hyperbolic tangent, exponential linear units, and SoftPlus activation. A brief overview of several important nonlinear activations are discussed in Sections 2.2.1–2.2.6.

3.2.4 Pooling Layer

A pooling layer reduces the spatial size of the representation, which is another integral task of the CNN. This step is done to pool or extract the important features from the output of a convolutional layer.

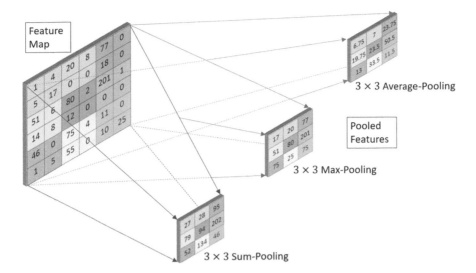

FIGURE 3.2 Schematic of Max, average, and sum pooling methods to remap the input features in a 3×3 array [40]. (From Tariq M. Arif, Introduction to Deep Learning for Engineers Using Python and Google Cloud Platform, 2020, Chap 4, Page 31, Springer Nature, with permission from Springer nature.)

The pooling process can reduce the spatial size or dimension of each feature map through different formulations such as max, average, sum, overlapping, L2, etc. This step generally helps the model to understand feature motifs that may appear at different locations of the training image. A schematic for feature mapping through max-pooling, average-pooling, and sum-pooling is given in Figure 3.2. Typically, the convolution neural network has several convolutional and pooling layers at the beginning before going through the fully connected layers. The pooling process in the neural network reduces the computational complexity and overfitting possibility.

3.2.5 Fully Connected Layer

The final stage of the CNN contains fully connected layers. It is similar to the regular artificial neural network and contains neurons that are connected to all neurons from the previous layer. The training image features that are extracted through convolutional and pooling layers are classified in the fully connected layer. Sometimes, to use computational memory efficiently, two small, fully connected layers are used instead of one large layer. Some of the popular convolution neural networks, such as AlexNet, and VGG Net, use more than one fully connected layer, followed by the output layer. The fully connected layers also use a

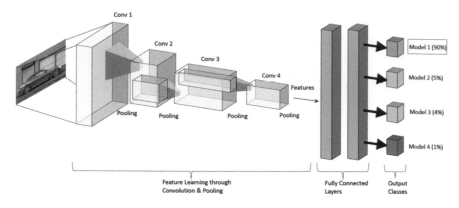

FIGURE 3.3   CNN transforms the input car image (RGB inputs) through convolutional, pooling, and fully connected layers. The output layer has softmax activation (for multi-class classification) to represent probability distribution for different car models. This example indicates that the car is in Model 1 class based on probability [40]. (From Tariq M. Arif, Introduction to Deep Learning for Engineers Using Python and Google Cloud Platform, 2020, Chap 4, Page 32, Springer Nature, with permission from Springer Nature.)

backpropagation algorithm to update the network's weights and biases. The properties of fully connected layers depend on the types of problems (e.g., classification or segmentation). It is important to note that, for classification and regression problems, another supervised algorithm known as Support Vector Machine (SVM) can also be used instead of fully connected layers.

At the end of the fully connected layer, a softmax activation function can be used for doing multi-class classification, where the probabilities of each class will always sum up to one. Figure 3.3 shows a general framework of a CNN for multi-class classification problems. This example illustrates that, after training over many images, a deep learning model can learn features to identify a car model based on the given input picture. If we have more than two classes (different car models), the softmax activation function or the SVM can be used in the last layer.

3.2.6 Output Layer

The final layer of CNN is the output layer that uses a function (e.g., softmax function for multi-class classification) to output the probabilities of each category or class. Each neuron in this layer outputs a value between 0 and 1, which indicates the probability of being in a certain class.

3.3 APPLICATIONS

Among the deep learning architectures, CNN is computationally expensive as it requires a large volume of training data to avoid overfitting. However, it found a wide range of applications in several domains that require visual inputs and demonstrated state-of-the-art performances. Some major applications of CNN are given in the following sections.

3.3.1 Image Classification

The CNN model proved to be very useful for image classification problems, where the challenge is to assign a label to an image or photograph from a set of classes. For instance, CNNs can be used in applications for identifying whether an image contains a horse or cow, or can be used in recognizing different models of cars. The practical applications of image classifications are numerous. Using a labeled dataset, the deep learning CNN model can learn to identify images of humans, animals, plants, and objects and can diagnose or categorize extremely complex medical images. In the following sections, several common CNN applications are discussed.

3.3.2 Object Detection

Object detection is an important application of CNN that identifies and classifies multiple objects within an image. Object detection algorithms typically produce a bounding box around objects and classify those. This has many practical applications in our daily lives, such as surveillance, self-driving cars, traffic flow analysis, etc.

3.3.3 Image Segmentation

CNNs used in image segmentation tasks require dividing images into multiple areas corresponding to different objects. In the image segmentation process, the CNN algorithm classifies every pixel of an image rather than the entire image. This type of pixel-wise classification is also known as semantic segmentation. Image segmentation has numerous applications in the field of satellite image analysis, autonomous driving, and medical imaging, where it is essential to locate specific regions of an image (e.g., identify flood areas, road curb areas, internal parts from MRI scans, locate tumor location, etc.).

When the image segmentation process not only does the pixel-wise classifications but also differentiates between different instances of the same objects, it is called instance segmentation. For example, if an image contains three flowers, semantic segmentation will label all pixels for flowers as one class, but the instance segmentation will identify and label each flower (flower type) separately.

3.3.4 Natural Language Processing (NLP)

Traditional CNN architectures are primarily used for image data analysis. However, there are variations of CNN that are used in NLP for tasks such as text classification, machine translation, and sentiment analysis. For example, in NLP, CNN can be used to scan through words in a sentence (1D grid) and can be trained to recognize key patterns.

3.3.5 Image Generation

CNN can be used to construct Generative Adversarial Networks (GAN) learning models. These models are typically used for generating artificial data or images using a generator and discriminator. In GAN, the generator uses random noises as input and utilizes CNN architecture to transform the noise into an image or data until it becomes indistinguishable from the real data. On the other hand, the discriminator compares the data (e.g., real image vs generated image) using CNN and classifies those using a binary classifier (True or False). Since in the training process, two networks are trying to compete with each other, it is also known as an adversarial network. The final goal of GAN is to produce images using a generator that the discriminator fails to distinguish from the real images of the dataset.

Some key applications of GAN include producing synthetic images and data when collecting actual data is very time-consuming, discovering new medicines through developing artificial molecule structures, producing high-resolution images, producing text descriptions from images, generating new design patterns for the fashion industry, creating new scenarios or characters in video games, etc.

CNNs are also applied in a wide variety of fields that use video streaming. Since videos are just sequences of images, using CNN, they can be analyzed for real-time object tracking, activity recognition, and face recognition. In many industries, CNNs are used to detect anomalies in the product during the visual inspection stage and to train on time series or volumetric data (3D) for various engineering tasks. The applications of CNN are not limited to the above-mentioned areas. Currently, CNN is being explored in a lot of different novel scientific and engineering fields. However, the success of implementing the CNN depends on the quality, quantity, and variations of available datasets as well as on the effectiveness of the deep learning or transfer learning models.

REFERENCES

1. Bhat, S. S., Ananth, A., and Venugopala, P. S., 2023, "Design and Evolution of Deep Convolutional Neural Networks in Image Classification: A Review," International Journal of Integrated Engineering, 15(1), pp. 213–225.
2. Kumar, B., Dikshit, O., Gupta, A., and Singh, M. K., 2020, "Feature Extraction for Hyperspectral Image Classification: A Review," International Journal of Remote Sensing, 41(16), pp. 6248–6287.
3. Chen, L., Li, S., Bai, Q., Yang, J., Jiang, S., and Miao, Y., 2021, "Review of Image Classification Algorithms Based on Convolutional Neural Networks," Remote Sensing, 13(22), p. 4712.
4. Sun, H., Zheng, X., Lu, X., and Wu, S., 2020, "Spectral-Spatial Attention Network for Hyperspectral Image Classification," IEEE Transactions on Geoscience and Remote Sensing, 58(5), pp. 3232–3245.
5. Xu, Y., Zhang, L., Du, B., and Zhang, F., 2018, "Spectral-Spatial Unified Networks for Hyperspectral Image Classification," IEEE Transactions on Geoscience and Remote Sensing, 56(10), pp. 5893–5909.
6. Meister, S., Wermes, M. A. M., Stüve, J., and Groves, R. M., 2021, "Review of Image Segmentation Techniques for Layup Defect Detection in the Automated Fiber Placement Process: A Comprehensive Study to Improve AFP Inspection," Journal of Intelligent Manufacturing, 32(8), pp. 2099–2119.
7. Shrivastava, N., and Bharti, J., 2020, "Automatic Seeded Region Growing Image Segmentation for Medical Image Segmentation: A Brief Review," International Journal of Image and Graphics, 20(3), p. 2050018.
8. Chen, C., Qin, C., Qiu, H., Tarroni, G., Duan, J., Bai, W., and Rueckert, D., 2020, "Deep Learning for Cardiac Image Segmentation: A Review," Frontiers in Cardiovascular Medicine, 7, p. 25.
9. Kumar, A., and Jain, S. K., 2022, "Deformable Models for Image Segmentation: A Critical Review of Achievements and Future Challenges," Computers & Mathematics With Applications, 119, pp. 288–311.
10. Liu, L., Wolterink, J. M., Brune, C., and Veldhuis, R. N. J., 2021, "Anatomy-Aided Deep Learning for Medical Image Segmentation: A Review," Physics in Medicine & Biology, 66(11), p. 11.
11. Xiao, Y., Tian, Z., Yu, J., Zhang, Y., Liu, S., Du, S., and Lan, X., 2020, "A Review of Object Detection Based on Deep Learning," Multimedia Tools and Applications, 79(33–34), pp. 23729–23791.
12. Zhao, Z.-Q., Zheng, P., Xu, S.-T., and Wu, X., 2019, "Object Detection With Deep Learning: A Review," IEEE Transaction on Neural Networks and Learning Systems, 30(11), pp. 3212–3232.
13. Kaur, R., and Singh, S., 2023, "A Comprehensive Review of Object Detection with Deep Learning," Digital Signal Processing, 132, p. 103812.
14. Ji, Y., Zhang, H., Zhang, Z., and Liu, M., 2021, "CNN-Based Encoder-Decoder Networks for Salient Object Detection: A Comprehensive Review and Recent Advances," Information Sciences, 546, pp. 835–857.
15. Li, L., Mu, X., Li, S., and Peng, H., 2020, "A Review of Face Recognition Technology," IEEE Access, 8, pp. 139110–139120.

16. Oloyede, M. O., Hancke, G. P., and Myburgh, H. C., 2020, "A Review on Face Recognition Systems: Recent Approaches and Challenges," Multimedia Tools and Applications, 79(37–38), pp. 27891–27922.

17. Ahmed, S. B., Ali, S. F., Ahmad, J., Adnan, M., and Fraz, M. M., 2020, "On the Frontiers of Pose Invariant Face Recognition: A Review," The Artificial Intelligence Review, 53(4), pp. 2571–2634.

18. Zhang, X., and Zhao, H., 2021, "Hyperspectral-Cube-Based Mobile Face Recognition: A Comprehensive Review," Information Fusion, 74, pp. 132–150.

19. Rani, S., Lakhwani, K., and Kumar, S., 2022, "Three Dimensional Objects Recognition & Pattern Recognition Technique; Related Challenges: A Review," Multimedia Tools and Applications, 81(12), pp. 17303–17346.

20. Zhang, X.-Y., Liu, C.-L., and Suen, C. Y., 2020, "Towards Robust Pattern Recognition: A Review," Proceedings of the IEEE, 108(6), pp. 894–922.

21. Bhamare, D., and Suryawanshi, P., 2018, "Review on Reliable Pattern Recognition With Machine Learning Techniques," Fuzzy Information and Engineering, 10(3), pp. 362–377.

22. Daly, C., 2018, "Chinese AI Beats Human Doctors in Diagnosing Brain Tumours," AI Business. https://aibusiness.com/verticals/chinese-ai-beats-human-doctors-in-diagnosing-brain-tumours

23. Vial, A., Stirling, D., Field, M., Ros, M., Ritz, C., Carolan, M., Holloway, L., and Miller, A. A., 2018, "The Role of Deep Learning and Radiomic Feature Extraction in Cancer-Specific Predictive Modelling: A Review," Translational Cancer Research, 7(3), pp. 803–816.

24. Craig, M., 2016, "AI System in Eye Scans Enables Better Diagnosis of Inherited Retinal Diseases," News Medical Lifes Sciences, Manchester, England.

25. Huang, X., Wang, H., She, C., Feng, J., Liu, X., Hu, X., Chen, L., and Tao, Y., 2022, "Artificial Intelligence Promotes the Diagnosis and Screening of Diabetic Retinopathy," Frontiers in Endocrinology, 13, p. 946915.

26. Swarnalatha, P., and Sevugan, P., 2018, Big Data Analytics for Satellite Image Processing and Remote Sensing, IGI Global, Hershey, PA.

27. Aminzadeh, F., Temizel, C., and Hajizadeh, Y., 2022, Artificial Intelligence and Data Analytics for Energy Exploration and Production, Wiley, Hoboken, NJ.

28. Lal, B., Bavoh, C. B., and Sayani, J. K. S., 2023, Machine Learning and Flow Assurance in Oil and Gas Production, Springer Nature, Switzerland.

29. Araújo, D., Couceiro, M. S., Seifert, L., Sarmento, H., and Davids, K., 2021, Artificial Intelligence in Sport Performance Analysis, Taylor & Francis, New York, NY.

30. Kim, J., Calhoun, V. D., Shim, E., and Lee, J. H., 2016, "Deep Neural Network With Weight Sparsity Control and Pre-Training Extracts Hierarchical Features and Enhances Classification Performance: Evidence from Whole-Brain Resting-State Functional Connectivity Patterns of Schizophrenia," NeuroImage, 124(Pt A), pp. 127–146.

31. Zhao, Y., Dong, Q., Zhang, S., Zhang, W., Chen, H., Jiang, X., Guo, L., Hu, X., Han, J., and Liu, T., 2018, "Automatic Recognition of fMRI-Derived Functional Networks Using 3-D Convolutional Neural Networks," IEEE Transactions on Bio-Medical Engineering, 65(9), pp. 1975–1984.

32. Jang, H., Plis, S. M., Calhoun, V. D., and Lee, J. H., 2017, "Task-Specific Feature Extraction and Classification of fMRI Volumes Using a Deep Neural Network Initialized with a Deep Belief Network: Evaluation Using Sensorimotor Tasks," NeuroImage, 145(Pt B), pp. 314–328.
33. Karimi-Rouzbahani, H., Bagheri, N., and Ebrahimpour, R., 2017, "Invariant Object Recognition is a Personalized Selection of Invariant Features in Humans, Not Simply Explained by Hierarchical Feed-Forward Vision Models," Scientific Reports, 7(1), p. 14402.
34. Zhang, B., 2010, "Computer Vision vs. Human Vision," 9th IEEE International Conference on Cognitive Informatics (ICCI'10), IEEE, p. 3.
35. Lecun, Y., Bottou, L., Bengio, Y., and Haffner, P., 1998, "Gradient-Based Learning Applied to Document Recognition," Proceedings of the IEEE, 86(11), pp. 2278–2324.
36. Kim, Y., 2014, "Convolutional Neural Networks for Sentence Classification," Proceedings of the 2014 Conference on Empirical Methods in Natural Language Processing.
37. Abdel-Hamid, O., Mohamed, A., Jiang, H., Deng, L., Penn, G., and Yu, D., 2014, "Convolutional Neural Networks for Speech Recognition," IEEE/ACM Transactions on Audio, Speech, and Language Processing, 22(10), pp. 1533–1545.
38. Ciregan, D., Meier, U., and Schmidhuber, J., 2012, "Multi-column deep neural networks for image classification," Proceedings of the 2012 IEEE Conference on Computer Vision and Pattern Recognition, IEEE, pp. 3642–3649.
39. Liu, X., Deng, Z., and Yang, Y., 2019, "Recent Progress in Semantic Image Segmentation," Artificial Intelligence Review, 52(2), pp. 1089–1106.
40. Arif, T. M., 2020, "Introduction to Deep Learning," Introduction to Deep Learning for Engineers: Using Python and Google Cloud Platform, Springer International Publishing, Cham, pp. 29–36.

## CHAPTER 4

Natural Language Processing Fundamentals

4.1 INTRODUCTION

Natural language processing (NLP) is a branch of artificial intelligence (AI) that enables human–computer interaction through natural language in a practical and understandable manner. Many different approaches are included in NLP to read, interpret, and understand human-level conversational and chatting skills. Some key tasks of NLP include the understanding of language or sentiment, interpreting images, and the generalization of tasks such as text summarizations.

Like other sub-fields of AI, NLP has experienced tremendous growth in the last decade. However, the core development of NLP can be dated back to the 1950s when rule-based systems were introduced by linguists for translations [1]. One of the early notable projects on this is the Georgetown-IBM experiment that translated sixty Russian sentences into the English language. During this time, the work of Noam Chomsky on transformational grammar revolutionized the scientific study of language and created a solid pathway for the future development of computational models [2]. In the early 1990s, statistical methods that can learn from data instead of using preset rules found their way to NLP [3, 4]. These developments in NLP were primarily for data-driven probabilistic models. One of the key milestones of that era was IBM's statistical machine translation system [5].

DOI: 10.1201/9781003402923-4

From the late 1990s to 2010, advanced machine-learning algorithms started to achieve enhanced performance due to the dramatic increase in computational power [6]. After 2010, deep learning algorithms flourished alongside high-performance GPU computing, and it drove significant advancements in NLP. During this time, the recurrent neural network (RNN) and Long Short-Term Memory (LSTP) gained popularity for interpreting data in the context of time [7]. In 2017, transformer-based models were proposed that revolutionized NLP implementations through state-of-the-art methods such as Bidirectional Transformers for Language Understanding (BERT) by Google, GPT (Generative Pre-trained Transformer) by OpenAI, Embeddings from Language Models (ELMo) by AllenNLP [8–11]. These transform models can be trained on very large datasets and be fine-tuned to accomplish certain goals with improved performance. Recently, Chat GPT-3.5 and 4 have set new milestones in this field by producing remarkable human-like answers.

The transformer-based models can also perform very sophisticated text generation, story summarizations, translations, etc. At the current pace of development, NLP systems are expected to be increasingly skillful and become accessible to everyday users. Most of the time, in NLP, RNN models are utilized to regulate, analyze, and recognize patterns from sequential data. The use of RNN in NLP escalated rapidly within the last decade. It has been delivering state-of-the-art results in many different fields, such as language processing, speech recognition, video analysis, fake video creation, music generation, grammatical inference, trajectory control of robots, and so on [12–18]. A brief overview of RNN architecture is presented in the following section.

4.2 RNN ARCHITECTURE

The RNN is a popular deep learning architecture that is used for predicting sequential data with the help of an additional memory state. RNN models have shown impressive performance in speech recognition and language translations. The internal structure of RNN process and pass data from one step to another through hidden layers. Therefore, the network's prediction depends on both current and past inputs, and also by considering outputs that have been assumed previously.

4.2.1 Basic Structures

RNN can be used in many different ways based on the nature of inputs and expected outputs. It deals with vectorized data, that is, inside this network, all inputs and outputs are vectors for many time steps. Among

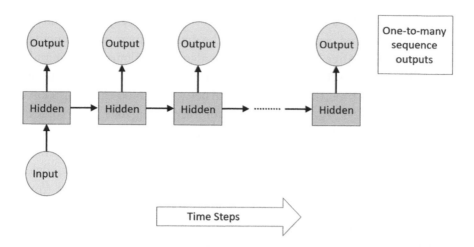

FIGURE 4.1   Schematic diagram of a one-to-many RNN architecture [19]. (From Tariq M. Arif, Introduction to Deep Learning for Engineers Using Python and Google Cloud Platform, 2020, Chap 4, Page 33, Springer Nature, with permission from Springer Nature.)

many underlying internal architectures of RNN, one-to-many, many-to-one, and many-to-many are commonly used.

For a one-to-many architecture, one input is mapped into multiple outputs (Figure 4.1). In this case, intermediate representations of the input unit are done in a series of hidden states, where every hidden state is a function of all previous states. An example application of this type of architecture is image captioning, where the input is a single image, but the outputs are a sequence of words describing the input.

In the many-to-one RNN architecture, many sequences of inputs are mapped into hidden states but produce only one class or quantity output. This type of network is very useful to gauge or classify the emotional state of a person and determine sensitivity scores from writings. A schematic of many-to-one RNN architecture is given in Figure 4.2.

In the many-to-many RNN structure, multiple inputs go through hidden states and produce multiple outputs. It is used for translating sentences into another language, video frame labeling, and many other prediction applications where multiple inputs produce multiple outputs. Many-to-many RNN structures might have different layouts based on the number of inputs and outputs. A schematic of many-to-many RNN architecture is given in Figure 4.3.

Besides these RNN architectures, there are many other input–output dynamics. For example, a simple one-to-one RNN structure similar to the classical feed-forward network.

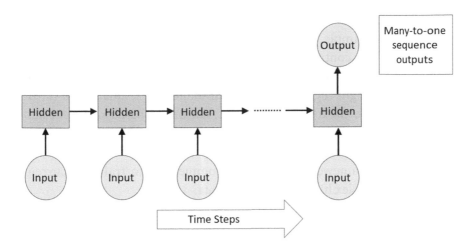

FIGURE 4.2 Schematic diagram of a many-to-one RNN architecture [19]. (From Tariq M. Arif, Introduction to Deep Learning for Engineers Using Python and Google Cloud Platform, 2020, Chap 4, Page 34, Springer Nature, with permission from Springer Nature.)

An RNN model is challenging to train because to update the parameters, the backpropagation algorithm needs to calculate gradients at different time steps. This operation can make the network unstable due to vanishing and exploding gradients. In order to avoid this problem, different supporting units such as gated recurrent unit (GRU), bidirectional

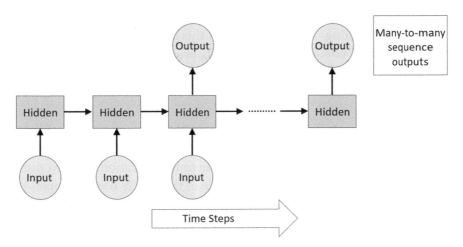

FIGURE 4.3 Schematic diagram of a many-to-many RNN architecture [19]. (From Tariq M. Arif, Introduction to Deep Learning for Engineers Using Python and Google Cloud Platform, 2020, Chap 4, Page 35, Springer Nature, with permission from Springer Nature.)

recurrent neural network (BRNN), and long-short-term memory (LSTM) are used. For example, the LSTM network uses cells with input, output, and forget-gate to control the flow of information. LSTM can be used with other tricks, such as gradient clipping to set a threshold value for the error gradient and weight regularization (L1-absolute or L2-squared) to introduce a penalty to the loss functions, etc. An LSTM-based recurrent network is more effective when several layers are involved in the sequence of data [13]. A GPU-based hardware (e.g., NVIDIA cuDNN) that supports deep learning frameworks is highly recommended to train a recurrent network for complex high-dimensional data.

4.3 APPLICATIONS

RNN architectures have a unique ability to retain information across time steps and thereby model sequential data. For this reason, it is widely used in various NLP applications such as machine translation, text generation, language modeling, etc. Although some RNNs, such as Elman Networks and Jordan Networks, found success during the 1990s they frequently experienced vanishing gradient issues for long-range dependencies. Later on, to address this issue, LSTM was proposed by Hochreiter and Schmidhuber in 1997 [20], and GRU was proposed in 2014 [21]. A few successful implementations of RNN are given in the following sections.

4.3.1 Time-Series Forecasting

RNN can be used to make prediction models when historical values are provided for training. A few examples in this area include the prediction of disease spread rate, population growth, price of a stock, weather forecasting, etc.

4.3.2 Text Processing

RNN and its variants (LSTM, GRU, etc.) are ideal for processing text data where the sequence of previous words is essential to perceive the context of a sentence. For this reason, there are numerous applications for text processing using RNN found around us. One of the widely used examples is Google's Neural Machine Translation (GNMT) which implements a deep LSTM network to translate languages [22]. It was introduced in 2016 and marked a breakthrough in machine translation as it transitioned from statistical models to machine learning models. GNMT was also a revolutionary milestone for Google due to its ability to translate languages that it hadn't been trained directly.

Besides machine translation, RNN is the key technology for generating synthetic texts for various applications. Some practical examples include generating automated replies for online customer care services, creating stories, generating news, generating novel poetry identical to certain poetic styles, etc.

4.3.3 Speech Recognition

RNN can model sequences of speech to convert those into text or specific commands. Therefore it is widely used in many automated services that use conversational speech for virtual assistant technology. Some typical applications are Google's voice search, Apple's Siri, Amazon's Alexa, Microsoft's Cortana, etc. Almost all of these can interactively communicate with users and are able to recognize the speaker's voice, speaking patterns, and command preferences. Besides these commercial applications, numerous RNN speech recognition algorithms are continuously emerging for more specialized applications.

4.3.4 Gesture Recognition

RNN has been used for recognizing gestures from video sequences in many virtual reality and gaming applications. Generally, RNN can be combined with CNN in these applications where CNN extracts high-level features from frames and RNN models the temporal dependencies. Gesture recognition also has a high potential for controlling machines, facilitating human–robot collaboration, and creating novel human–computer interaction applications. For example, in autonomous cars, pedestrian gestures can be used to predict their next course of movement and control the vehicle's speed accordingly. Many other gesture-based research achieved milestones that use RNN or a combination of CNN and RNN for advanced applications such as converting sign language to speech or summarizing a command text. More natural and intuitive RNN implementation through gesture recognition is continuously being explored by researchers.

4.3.5 Sentiment Analysis

RNN can be used to extract sentiment or emotional state from a piece of writing, news, or social media posts. It can rate an item using a scale (e.g., five being highly agree and zero being highly disagree) or using standard sentiments such as positive, negative, or neutral. Modern e-commerce or online retail stores use this model to analyze customer reviews and monitor their brand success through social media engagements.

Wide-ranging applications of RNNs are continuously being explored as people are increasingly involved in online searches and advertisements. A few recent examples include stock price forecasting using updated social media posts and news sentiment, analyzing tweets and trends for political campaigns, prioritizing customer support by analyzing messages, detecting patient's moods by analyzing mental health apps on cell phones, etc.

RNN examples presented in Section 4.3 represent a small fraction of its overall uses. Many other fields will likely experience the advancements of NLP and RNN. A few possible enhancements are expected in the field of personalized robotic assistance, improved accessibility for disabled and elderly persons, real-time translation, and smart home or IoT systems. As AI are likely to integrate more into our daily life, the impact of RNN will be significant in the near future.

4.4 OTHER DEEP LEARNING MODELS

Among the other deep learning models, recursive and unsupervised pre-trained Networks are gaining popularity. Recursive networks apply same set of weights recursively to learn from structured information, and it is known for being computationally expensive [23]. Recursive models are suitable for pattern analysis as they can process both the numerical and symbolic data together. Different variants of state-of-the-art recursive networks are continuously emerging with the help of contemporary researchers. Although it is relatively less popular than the recurrent network, it has shown excellent performance in NLP, image decomposition, and forecasting problems.

Generative Adversarial Networks (GANs) are one of the exciting deep learning classes. The GAN can produce realistic data by using two parallel adversarial networks that compete with each other. One of the networks works as a data generator, and the other network classifies it by utilizing real data. This process continues until the second network fails to discriminate between the real and synthetic data [24]. A GAN model is relatively difficult to train as it can suffer from mode collapse, diminished gradient, and non-convergence problems [25, 26]. Generative networks can be used to generate realistic pictures or images, and it is explored in many different engineering domains for image reconstruction. Recently, GAN was used to learn scene dynamics from a large amount of unlabeled video (26 terabytes), and it also showed impressive results in recovering features from astrophysical images by reducing random and systematic noises [27].

Although GAN is an amazing development for deep learning, using it, people can make fake media content, realistic images, and online profiles that can negatively affect our society. There are numerous other potential applications of GAN that exist in the fields of arts, industry, and medicine, and it will definitely create an impact on our society in the near future.

REFERENCES

1. Hutchins, W. J., 1995, "Machine Translation: A Brief History," Concise History of the Language Sciences, E. F. K. Koerner, and R. E. Asher, eds., Pergamon, Amsterdam, pp. 431–445.
2. Dunne, L., 2023, "Noam Chomsky's Radical Approach to Language," https://www.thecollector.com/noam-chomsky-radical-approach-to-language/.
3. Manning, C., and Schutze, H., 1999, Foundations of Statistical Natural Language Processing, MIT Press, Cambridge, England.
4. Nivre, J., 2001, "On statistical methods in natural language processing," Proceedings of the 13th Nordic Conference of Computational Linguistics (NODALIDA 2001). https://aclanthology.org/W01-1720/
5. Apte, C., Morgenstern, L., and Hong, S. J., 2000, "AI at IBM Research," IEEE Intelligent Systems and Their Applications, 15(6), pp. 51–57.
6. Johri, P., Khatri, S. K., Al-Taani, A. T., Sabharwal, M., Suvanov, S., and Kumar, A., 2020, "Natural language processing: History, evolution, application, and future work," Proceedings of 3rd International Conference on Computing Informatics and Networks: ICCIN 2020, Springer, pp. 365–375.
7. Fang, W., Chen, Y., and Xue, Q., 2021, "Survey on Research of RNN-Based Spatio-Temporal Sequence Prediction Algorithms," Journal on Big Data, 3(3), p. 97.
8. Gillioz, A., Casas, J., Mugellini, E., and Abou Khaled, O., 2020, "Overview of the Transformer-based Models for NLP Tasks," 2020 15th Conference on Computer Science and Information Systems (FedCSIS), IEEE, pp. 179–183.
9. Nath, S., Marie, A., Ellershaw, S., Korot, E., and Keane, P. A., 2022, "New Meaning for NLP: The Trials and Tribulations of Natural Language Processing with GPT-3 in Ophthalmology," British Journal of Ophthalmology, 106(7), pp. 889–892.
10. Rothman, D., 2021, Transformers for Natural Language Processing: Build Innovative Deep Neural Network Architectures for NLP with Python, PyTorch, TensorFlow, BERT, RoBERTa, and More, Packt Publishing Ltd, Birmingham, UK.
11. Laskar, M. T. R., Huang, X., and Hoque, E., 2020, "Contextualized Embeddings Based Transformer Encoder for Sentence Similarity Modeling in Answer Selection Task," Proceedings of the Twelfth Language Resources and Evaluation Conference, European Language Resources Association, pp. 5505–5514.
12. Li, X., and Wu, X., 2014, "Constructing Long Short-Term Memory based Deep Recurrent Neural Networks for Large Vocabulary Speech Recognition." https://arxiv.org/abs/1410.4281

13. Graves, A., Mohamed, A., and Hinton, G., 2013, "Speech Recognition With Deep Recurrent Neural Networks," Proceedings 2013 IEEE International Conference on Acoustics, Speech and Signal Processing, IEEE, pp. 6645–6649.

14. Güera, D., and Delp, E. J., 2018, "Deepfake video detection using recurrent neural networks," 2018 15th IEEE International Conference on Advanced Video and Signal Based Surveillance (AVSS), IEEE, pp. 1–6.

15. Marinescu, A.-I., 2019, "Bach 2.0 - Generating Classical Music Using Recurrent Neural Networks," Procedia Computer Science, 159, pp. 117–124.

16. Eck, D., and Schmidhuber, J., 2002, "Learning the Long-Term Structure of the Blues," Proc. Artificial Neural Networks—ICANN 2002, J. R. Dorronsoro, ed., Springer, Berlin Heidelberg, pp. 284–289.

17. Lawrence, S., Giles, C. L., and Fong, S., 2000, "Natural Language Grammatical Inference With Recurrent Neural Networks," Knowledge and Data Engineering, IEEE Transactions, 12, pp. 126–140.

18. Zhang, M.-J, and Chu, Z.-Z, 2012, "Adaptive Sliding Mode Control Based on Local Recurrent Neural Networks for Underwater Robot," Ocean Engineering, 45, pp. 56–62.

19. Arif, T. M., 2020, "Introduction to Deep Learning," Introduction to Deep Learning for Engineers: Using Python and Google Cloud Platform, Springer International Publishing, Cham, pp. 29–36.

20. Hochreiter, S., and Schmidhuber, J., 1997, "Long Short-Term Memory," Neural Computation, 9(8), pp. 1735–1780.

21. Chung, J., Gulcehre, C., Cho, K., and Bengio, Y., 2014, "Empirical evaluation of gated recurrent neural networks on sequence modeling," https://arxiv.org/abs/1412.3555

22. Wu, Y., Schuster, M., Chen, Z., Le, Q., Norouzi, M., Macherey, W., Krikun, M., Cao, Y., Gao, Q., Macherey, K., Klingner, J., Shah, A., Johnson, M., Liu, X., Kaiser, U, Gouws, S., Kato, Y., Kudo, T., Kazawa, H., and Dean, J., 2016, "Google's Neural Machine Translation System: Bridging the Gap between Human and Machine Translation." https://arxiv.org/abs/1609.08144

23. Chinea Manrique de Lara, A., 2009, "Understanding the Principles of Recursive Neural Networks: A Generative Approach to Tackle Model Complexity." https://arxiv.org/abs/0911.3298

24. Aggarwal, C. C., 2018, Neural Networks and Deep Learning: A Textbook, Springer International Publishing, Berlin.

25. Hui, J., 2018, "GAN—Why it is so hard to train Generative Adversarial Networks!," https://medium.com/@jonathan_hui/gan-why-it-is-so-hard-to-train-generative-advisory-networks-819a86b3750b.

26. Hong, Y., 2019, "Comparison of Generative Adversarial Networks Architectures Which Reduce Mode Collapse." https://arxiv.org/abs/1910.04636

27. Schawinski, K., Zhang, C., Zhang, H., Fowler, L., and Santhanam, G. K., 2017, "Generative Adversarial Networks Recover Features in Astrophysical Images of Galaxies Beyond the Deconvolution Limit," Monthly Notices of the Royal Astronomical Society: Letters, 467(1), pp. L110–L114.

## CHAPTER 5

Deep Learning Framework Installation

Pytorch and Cuda

5.1 INTRODUCTION TO DEEP LEARNING FRAMEWORKS

Deep learning has many different popular frameworks that have experienced explosive growth in recent years. Most of these frameworks are developed and supported by prominent tech companies such as Google, Microsoft, Facebook, and scientific research teams from various organizations. One of the prime catalysts for the growth in this field is that all of the standard deep learning frameworks, as well as associated software and library packages, are open-source and free to use. Besides the availability through open-sourced licenses, there are numerous active online question-and-answer and discussion platforms such as Quora (https://www.quora.com/), Stack Overflow (https://stackoverflow.com/), Stack Exchange (https://stackexchange.com/), Reddit (https://stackexchange.com/), etc., that are indirectly supporting these newly developed frameworks and propelling the growth of AI and deep learning.

As of now, a few popular deep learning frameworks are TensorFlow by Google's Brain Team [1], PyTorch by Adam et al. [2], Keras by Chollet et al. [3], Caffe by Berkely Artificial Intelligence Research [4], and Microsoft Cognitive Toolkit (CNTK) by Microsoft Research [5]. Additionally, there are a couple of other frameworks or sub-frameworks, such as Theano, DL4J, Sonnet, Chainer, MXNet, Gluon, ONNX, etc., that are growing fast in adoptions [6–11]. It is not correct to declare the superiority of a framework over others, as all of these are supported by active developers, scientists, and research communities. There are both advantages and disadvantages to using one framework over another, and depending on the use case, one framework can be preferable over others. For example, TensorFlow has many deep learning libraries with scalability and advanced visualization features, but it has relatively low speed and limited Graphical Processing Unit (GPU) support. On the other hand, the python-friendly PyTorch is easier to learn and has strong community support, but doesn't have good visualization features like TensorBoard.

In this book, all of the case studies (Chapters 6–9) and programming codes are given in PyTorch. One of the main reasons for using PyTorch is that it is comparatively less challenging to learn for newcomers who have familiarity with Python programming. PyTorch also supports dynamic computation graphs that allow users to debug code in a convenient way by running smaller sections. In the following sections, we are going to present the PyTorch framework setups and related library package installations in a workstation with multiple and single Nvidia graphics cards.

5.2 ANACONDA INSTALLATION

Anaconda is one of the most common Python distributions with a great collection of scientific packages, libraries, tools, and Interactive Development Environments (IDEs) for data scientists. One of the advantages of using Anaconda is its ability to create environments for various versions of Pythons and manage installed packages within that environment. Anaconda installation automatically includes hundreds of libraries such as "matpolotlib", "bokeh", "seoborn", "numpy", "mkl", "pandas", "scipy", "pillow", "scikit-learn", etc., and also include interactive Python programming environments such as Spyder, Jupyter Notebook, JupyterLab, PyCharm, R Studio, etc. Anaconda has an exceptionally large data science community whose members regularly post ideas, update packages, and write blogs to share their skills.

All the example codes in this book are written and executed using a popular Python editor called Spyder IDE. Besides a regular editor for writing scripts, Spyder has an IPython console to execute commands, a variable explorer pane to examine data, a plots pane to show static figures, tools for code inspection, and much more. If Spyder IDE is launched from the Anaconda Command Prompt or Anaconda Navigator interface, it will be able to fetch all the packages installed in the Anaconda environment.

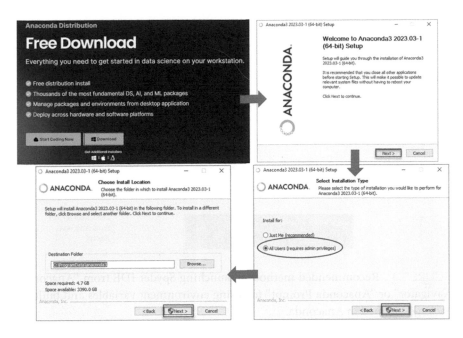

FIGURE 5.1   Download the Anaconda installer and run it using admin privileges.

First, we need to download the Anaconda installer from https://www.anaconda.com/download and run it using admin privileges (Figure 5.1).

During the installation process, make sure to check the "Register Anaconda3 as the system Python 3.10" and "Clear the package cache upon completion" options in the advanced installation option and proceed as shown in Figure 5.2. The Spyder IDE can be launched in two different ways in Windows: 1) search and open "Anaconda Navigator" from the search bar

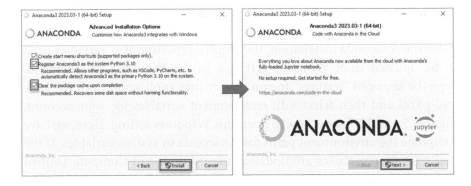

FIGURE 5.2   Check the "Register Anaconda3 as the system Python 3.10" and "Clear the package cache upon completion" options during the installation process.

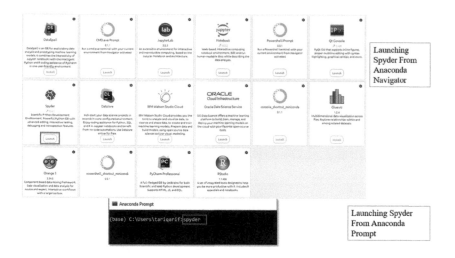

FIGURE 5.3   Recommended method of launching Spyder IDE from "Anaconda Navigator" or "Anaconda Prompt" for using environment variables and built-in packages defined in Anaconda.

and press the Spyder's launch button, and 2) search and open "Anaconda Prompt" from the Windows search bar and enter the command "spyder" (Figure 5.3). Both of these opening methods are recommended, as opening Spyder from the desktop or the program menu's shortcut may not find all the environment variables assigned in Anaconda environment.

In some workstations, running Spyder from the Windows shortcut (from the program menu or desktop's shortcut) may find all the variables and library packages, but it depends on the permission level that the user has. However, it is always recommended to launch Spyder IDE using the methods shown in Figure 5.3.

5.3 SETTING UP ENVIRONMENT VARIABLES

After the Anaconda installation, the required environment variables need to be updated from Windows settings. In the Windows search menu, type the keyword "settings" to run the settings application from the control panel and then select Edit environment variables for your account. Figures 5.4 and 5.5 show how to open this Windows setting. Here, we have to update the environment paths for Anaconda in system variables. If the paths for user variables are updated, the PyTorch and Compute Unified Device Architecture (CUDA) toolkit will be installed properly only for one specific user. Therefore, it is convenient to update system variables instead of user variables.

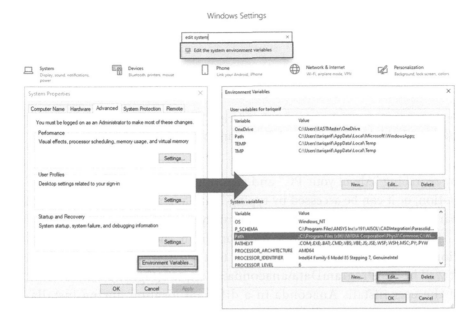

FIGURE 5.4   Edit system environment variables for adding Anaconda paths.

If the edit user variables application is launched, the edition option of the system variables will be disabled. In that case, we will need to confirm (or reassign) the admin privileges of the current user and try editing the variables using any of the two options shown in Figure 5.5. The system's environment variables can be accessed from Windows setting

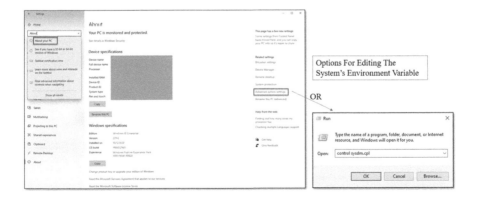

FIGURE 5.5   Edit System's Environment variables from Windows setting by searching "About your PC" and selecting the "Advanced System Settings" option or by typing "run" application from the search bar and executing the command "control sysdm.cpl".

FIGURE 5.6 Copy the location for the "Scripts" folder from the Anaconda installation and add this to the System's Environment variable "Path" (Figure 5.4).

by searching "About your PC" and selecting "Advanced System Settings" option, or it can be accessed by typing "run" application from the search bar and executing the command "control sysdm.cpl".

Next, the "Scripts" folder location from the Anaconda installation needs to be copied and added to the environment. By default, it will be "C:\ProgramData\anaconda3\Scripts" (Figure 5.6). However, if the user installs Anaconda in a different location during installation (Figure 5.1), it will be based on the installed location. Also, the "ProgramData" folder inside the "C" drive might be hidden. In that case, show hidden items option needs to be checked from the Windows folder's "view" option.

When the "Edit" option is selected for the "Path" variable (Figure 5.4), another window will appear to add new paths. We have to add both "C:\ProgramData\anaconda3\Scripts" and "C:\ProgramData\anaconda3", and press "OK" in all Windows to apply this system settings (Figure 5.7). If "OK"s are not pressed, the settings will not be updated.

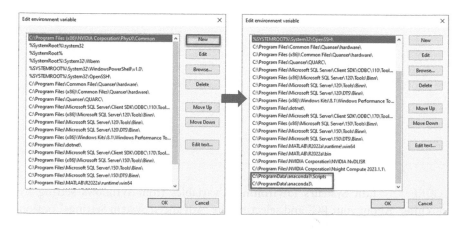

FIGURE 5.7 Update the system's environment variable path to add the location of the Anaconda installation folder and "Scripts" folder.

5.4 INSTALL AND SETUP PYTORCH FRAMEWORK

In this section, the deep learning framework PyTorch installation and related setup procedures are explained. Before the installation, it is important to check for any latest driver updates for the graphics card. This update option can be found by launching "Device Manager" from the Windows search menu and right-clicking the GPU name under device adapters. We also need to make sure the GPU is CUDA compatible, which is a parallel computing and programming model to increase the computing performance of GPUs. Nvidia GPUs (GeForce, Quadro, and Tesla) and Grid solutions support CUDA accelerated applications, and a complete list of CUDA GPUs is found at [12]. The case studies presented in this book use a workstation with two Nvidia GeForce RTX3090 GPUs to demonstrate how to run a deep learning model on a multi-GPU workstation. Also, the case study shows examples of running models in a workstation with a single Nvidia Quadro P1000 GPU. Both of the GPU types that we used support CUDA applications.

Next, the PyTorch framework needs to be installed for a stable CUDA version, which is currently released up to the CUDA 11.8 platform (as of July 2023). PyTorch's site provides various ways to install PyTorch for different packages and programming languages. From PyTorch's site [13], installation commands for the stable CUDA 11.8 version through the conda package manager can be found by selecting the options shown in Figure 5.8. In the near future, if a stable CUDA 12.x is released for PyTorch, we may install that version instead.

Save the command line from Figure 5.8 for installing PyTorch. After this, install or update "pywin32" to access Windows API functions on Python (Figure 5.9).

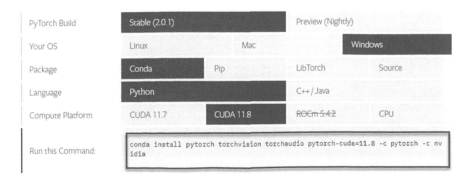

FIGURE 5.8   Select the options from [13] (https://pytorch.org/get-started/locally/) and copy the command for PyTorch installation for a stable CUDA version.

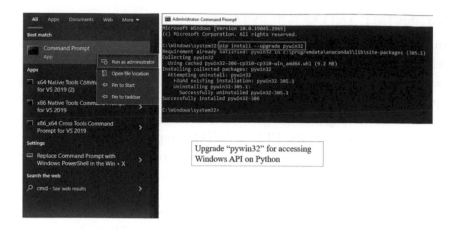

FIGURE 5.9   Run the "Command Prompt" as administrator and update "pywin32".

Next, go to the "Scripts" folder by accessing Anaconda's installation location using the command "cd C:\ProgramData\anaconda3\Scripts" and activate the root by typing "activate root" command (Figure 5.10). At this point, we may check key information related to current conda package by using the command "conda info". In the information, make sure that the base environment of the Anaconda is writable.

FIGURE 5.10   Activate root and check conda package information from the "Scripts" folder.

Install PyTorch from "Anaconda Prompt" as administrator

FIGURE 5.11   Run "Anaconda Prompt" as administrator and enter PyTorch installation commands copied from PyTorch's installation site (Figure 5.8).

Now, open the "Anaconda Prompt" from the menu by searching it and execute the installation command that was copied for PyTorch installation in Figure 5.8. If the "base" is not active in Anaconda Prompt, enter "conda activate" to activate it before installing the PyTorch. The PyTorch will collect packages and will try to solve environments for some time, as shown in Figure 5.11.

As the installation progresses, the command window will display the packages to be updated and will ask for permission to proceed. After entering "y" to proceed, it will download and install packages and libraries and, finally, will show "done" for preparing, verifying, and executing transactions (Figure 5.12). This indicates that the installation process is completed correctly. However, if one of these transactions shows "failed" and an error message says, "The current user does not have write permissions to the target environment", it indicates that the installation is incomplete.

The permission error shown in Figure 5.13 may happen even if the user is one of the admins of the workstation. To resolve this issue, go to the Anaconda installation folder (in our case, it is C:\ProgramData\anaconda3) and right-click the "anaconda3" folder to access properties. In the properties, allow full permissions for the domain user (or the current user) by checking all the "Allow" options and pressing "OK". This will enable the user to make any changes to the installation folder. After allowing all permissions, PyTorch should be uninstalled from the controls panel's programs and FEATURES or uninstaller applications (only if it wasn't installed correctly, as shown in Figure 5.12). It is highly recommended to uninstall PyTorch using the free "Revo Uninstaller Pro" software, as it will clean any files or Windows registry entries that remain from the previous installation [14]. Then PyTorch can be installed again using Anaconda Prompt, as shown in Figure 5.11.

FIGURE 5.12   PyTorch installation in conda environment. Here, at the end of a successful installation, the "Anaconda Prompt" window will show "done" for preparing, verifying, and executing transactions.

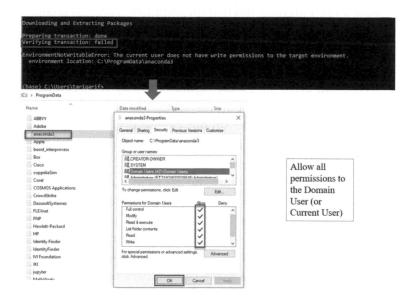

FIGURE 5.13   Allow all permissions to the domain user (or any current user) by checking all the "Allow" options and by pressing "OK".

5.4.1 CUDA and cuDNN Installation

The next major step is CUDA and CUDA Deep Neural Network library (cuDNN) installation in the workstation. The cuDNN library is built on top of the CUDA framework for high-performance machine learning or deep learning tasks. cuDNN also has optimized kernels for many popular computer vision and speech models. It can be used with TensorFlow, PyTorch, Torch, Caffe, Caffe2, Chainer, CNTK, Matlab, mxnet, paddlepaddle, and WolframLangugage [15]. Prior to CUDA installation, Python won't be able to use GPU for deep learning frameworks. In the console of Spyder IDE, if we import "torch" and check for CUDA using the command "torch.cuda.is_available()", it will return False (Figure 5.14).

The CUDA program requires Microsoft's Visual Studio development toolkit for using C++ compilers in Windows. The correct version of Visual Studio can be checked from the cuDNN support matrix at [16] (Figure 5.15), and for Windows, we find that Visual Studio 2019 needs to be installed for CUDA 11.8 (PyTorch's CUDA platform is 11.8 in Figure 5.8).

More detailed instructions for CUDA installation are available on Nvidia's official website [17].

We can download the older versions of Visual Studios from https://visualstudio.microsoft.com/vs/older-downloads/. A free Microsoft account needs to be created to download the Visual Studio installer from the dropdown menu under 2019 (Figure 5.16).

```
In [1]: import torch

In [2]: torch.cuda.is_available()
Out[2]: False
```

FIGURE 5.14 PyTorch framework cannot find CUDA before the cuDNN installation.

2.2. Windows

Windows 10 and Windows Server 2019 and 2016 are supported. Refer to the following table to view the list of supported Visual Studio versions for cuDNN.

Table 3. Visual Studio Versions Based on Your Version of CUDA

	CUDA 12.x - 11.8	CUDA 11.7 - 11.0
Visual Studio	2019	2017

FIGURE 5.15 Visual Studio 2019 is compatible with PyTorch's CUDA 11.8.

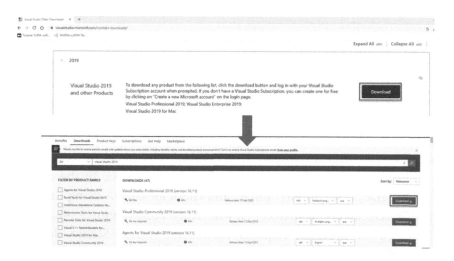

FIGURE 5.16 Create a Microsoft account and download the "Visual Studio Professional 2019" installer.

From the download location, once the Visual Studio installer is launched, select ".NET desktop development" and "Desktop development with C++" and press "install", to install these packages with the Visual Studio core installations (Figure 5.17). If the Visual Studio professional was already installed in the workstation, the "modify" button will appear instead of "install". In that case, make sure to hit "modify" to apply any updates.

After installing Visual Studio Professional 2019, download the CUDA toolkit installer by selecting the appropriate architecture and version for

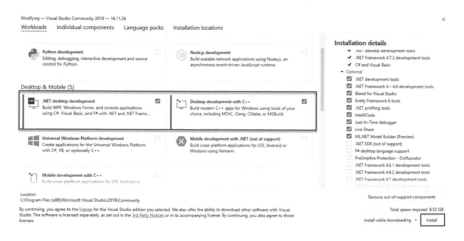

FIGURE 5.17 Select ".NET desktop development" and "Desktop development with C++" to install these packages with the Visual Studio 2019 core installation.

Operating System	Linux	Windows		
Architecture	x86_64			
Version	10	11	Server 2019	Server 2022
Installer Type	exe (local)	exe (network)		

Download Installer for Windows 11 x86_64

The base installer is available for download below.

> Base Installer — Download (3.2 GB) ⬇

Installation Instructions:

1. Double click cuda_12.1.1_531.14_windows.exe
2. Follow on-screen prompts

FIGURE 5.18   Download the CUDA installer by selecting the appropriate architecture and version.

Windows (Figure 5.18). This download page is at https://developer.nvidia.com/cuda-downloads.

Once the Nvidia CUDA toolkit installer (cuda_12.1.1_531.14_windows.exe) is downloaded, it can be launched from the download location. This installation process is very straightforward and can be completed by agreeing with the license agreement and pressing "Next"s. Some of these installation steps are shown in Figure 5.19.

Next, the cuDNN library needs to be downloaded for PyTorch's CUDA version. We can find the correct version using the cuDNN support matrix published in [16] and download the cuDNN using the option "Download

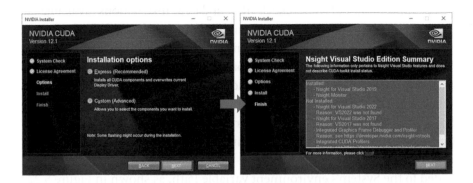

FIGURE 5.19   Install CUDA by launching the "cuda_12.1.1_531.14_windows.exe" installer.

cuDNN Download

NVIDIA cuDNN is a GPU-accelerated library of primitives for deep neural networks.

☑ I Agree To the Terms of the cuDNN Software License Agreement

Note: Please refer to the Installation Guide for release prerequisites, including supported GPU architectures and compute capabilities, before downloading.

For more information, refer to the cuDNN Developer Guide, Installation Guide and Release Notes on the Deep Learning SDK Documentation web page.

Download cuDNN v8.9.2 (June 1st, 2023), for CUDA 12.x

Download cuDNN v8.9.2 (June 1st, 2023), for CUDA 11.x

Local Installers for Windows and Linux, Ubuntu(x86_64, armsbsa)

Local Installer for Windows (Zip)

Local Installer for Linux x86_64 (Tar)

Local Installer for Linux PPC (Tar)

Local Installer for Linux SBSA (Tar)

Local Installer for Debian 11 (Deb)

Local Installer for Ubuntu18.04 x86_64 (Deb)

Local Installer for Ubuntu20.04 x86_64 (Deb)

Local Installer for Ubuntu22.04 x86_64 (Deb)

Local Installer for Ubuntu20.04 aarch64sbsa (Deb)

FIGURE 5.20   Download cuDNN library for Windows local installation.

cuDNN" from [18]. For this download, a sign-up or registration is required using an email address at the Nvidia Developers Program (https://developer.nvidia.com/developer-program). Nvidia will send an email to verify the account, and during the login process, Nvidia will also send out a verification link to that email address to approve the login request. From the cuDNN download page, check to Agree with the terms of the cuDNN License Agreement, select the latest release for CUDA 11.x, and then download the "Local Installer for Windows (zip)" file (Figure 5.20).

For installing cuDNN, check the updated instructions available at https://docs.nvidia.com/deeplearning/cudnn/install-guide/index.html. First, install the Zlib data compression library as shown in Figure 5.21. For most browsers, this file won't download automatically. Users should right-click and press "Save link as…" to download the "zlib123dllx64" zip file. There is another Zlib file given on the installation page for 32-bit workstations. Then we have to unzip this folder and save it in any local drive or directory (e.g., Figure 5.21 shows that the unzipped folder is saved in the C drive).

For this Zlib to work, the location of the "zlibwapi.dll" file needs to be added to the System's environment variable Path, as shown in Figure 5.22. To edit and add this new path to the system variables, follow the procedure shown in Figures 5.4 and 5.5.

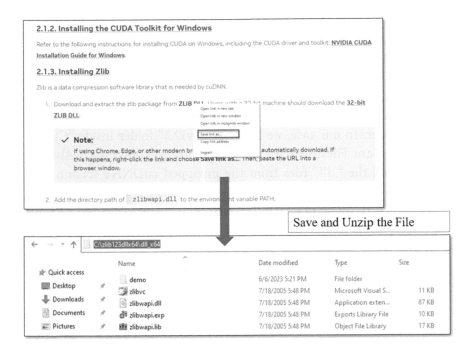

2.1.2. Installing the CUDA Toolkit for Windows

Refer to the following instructions for installing CUDA on Windows, including the CUDA driver and toolkit: **NVIDIA CUDA Installation Guide for Windows**.

2.1.3. Installing Zlib

Zlib is a data compression software library that is needed by cuDNN.

1. Download and extract the zlib package from **ZLIB DLL**. Users with a 32-bit machine should download the **32-bit ZLIB DLL**.

   ✓ **Note:**
   If using Chrome, Edge, or other modern br... automatically download. If this happens, right-click the link and choose **Save link as...**. Then, paste the URL into a browser window.

2. Add the directory path of `zlibwapi.dll` to the environment variable PATH.

Save and Unzip the File

FIGURE 5.21 Download the Zlib data compression file "zlib123dllx64.zip" for Windows, and save the unzipped folder "zlib123dllx64" in a local drive or directory.

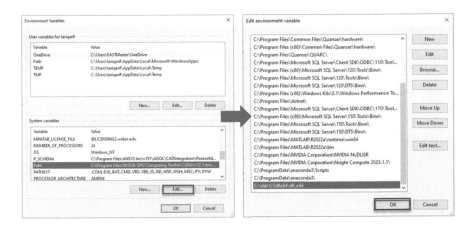

FIGURE 5.22 Update the system's environment variables Path and add the location of the "zlibwapi.dll" file.

The next step is installing cuDNN using the downloaded local installer zip file for Windows (Figure 5.20). To do this, first we have to unzip the cuDNN package containing "bin", "include", and "lib" folders. Then locate the CUDA installation folder in "ProgramFiles" that also have "bin", "include", and "folders". If the workstation has CUDA 11.x installed, then we will need to access the folder for that version (e.g., v11.x) inside the "CUDA" folder. In our case, we locate the "v12.1" folder inside "CUDA" (e.g., C:\Program Files\NVIDIA GPU Computing Toolkit\CUDA\v12.1). Now, copy all the ".dll" files from the unzipped cuDNN's (cudnn-windows-x86_64-8.9.0.131_cuda11-archive) "bin" folder and paste those into the located "bin" folder of CUDA installation (C:\Program Files\NVIDIA GPU Computing Toolkit\CUDA\v12.1\bin). Figure 5.23 shows this copy–paste step in our workstation.

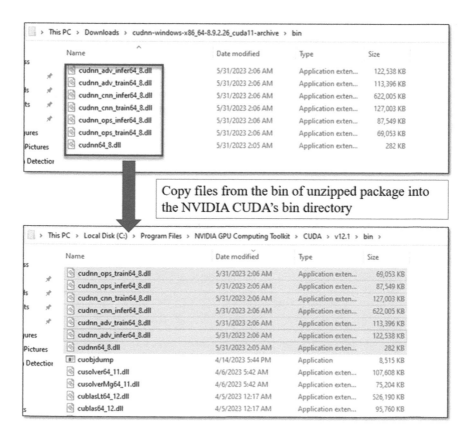

FIGURE 5.23 Copy all the ".dll" files from unzipped cuDNN's "bin" and paste those into the CUDA installation's "bin" directory.

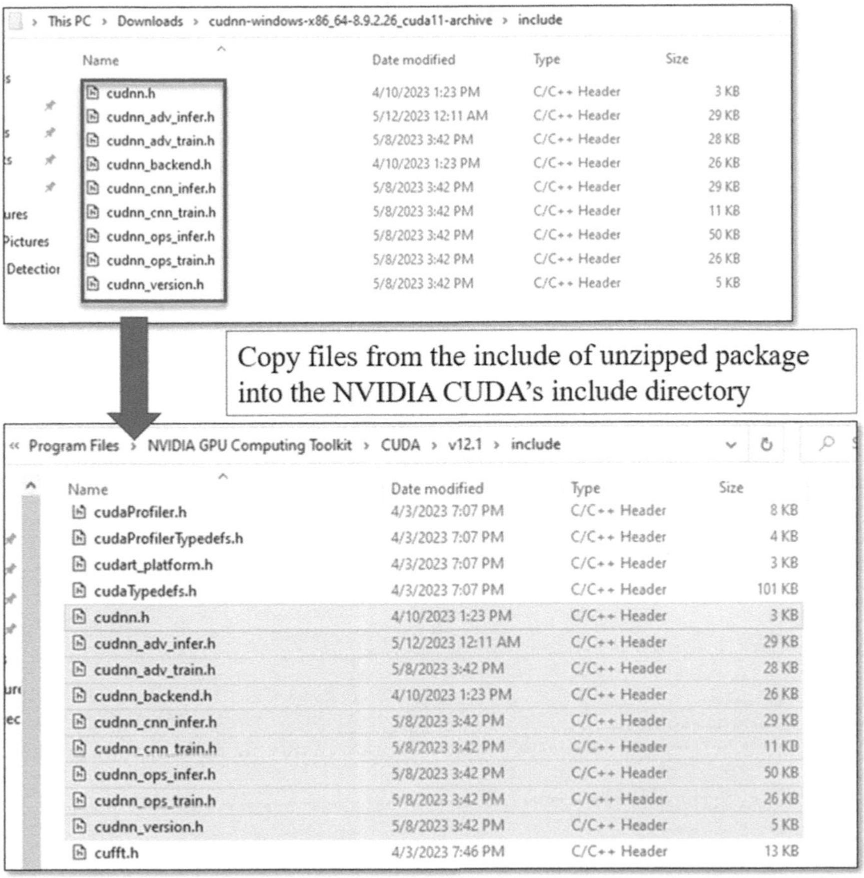

FIGURE 5.24 Copy all the ".h" files from unzipped cuDNN's "include" and paste those into the CUDA installation's "include" directory.

The same procedures have to be followed for copying all header and library files of cuDNN. We have to copy all the header ".h" files from the unzipped cuDNN's (cudnn-windows-x86_64-8.9.0.131_cuda11-archive) "include" folder and paste those into the "include" folder of CUDA installation (C:\Program Files\NVIDIA GPU Computing Toolkit\CUDA\v12.1\ include) as shown in Figure 5.24.

Next, copy all the library ".lib" files from the unzipped cuDNN's (cudnn-windows-x86_64-8.9.0.131_cuda11-archive) "….\lib\x64" folder and paste those into the "…\lib\x64" folder of CUDA installation (C:\Program Files\ NVIDIA GPU Computing Toolkit\CUDA\v12.1\lib\x64). Figures 5.23–5.25 are examples to show file locations, and readers may have different

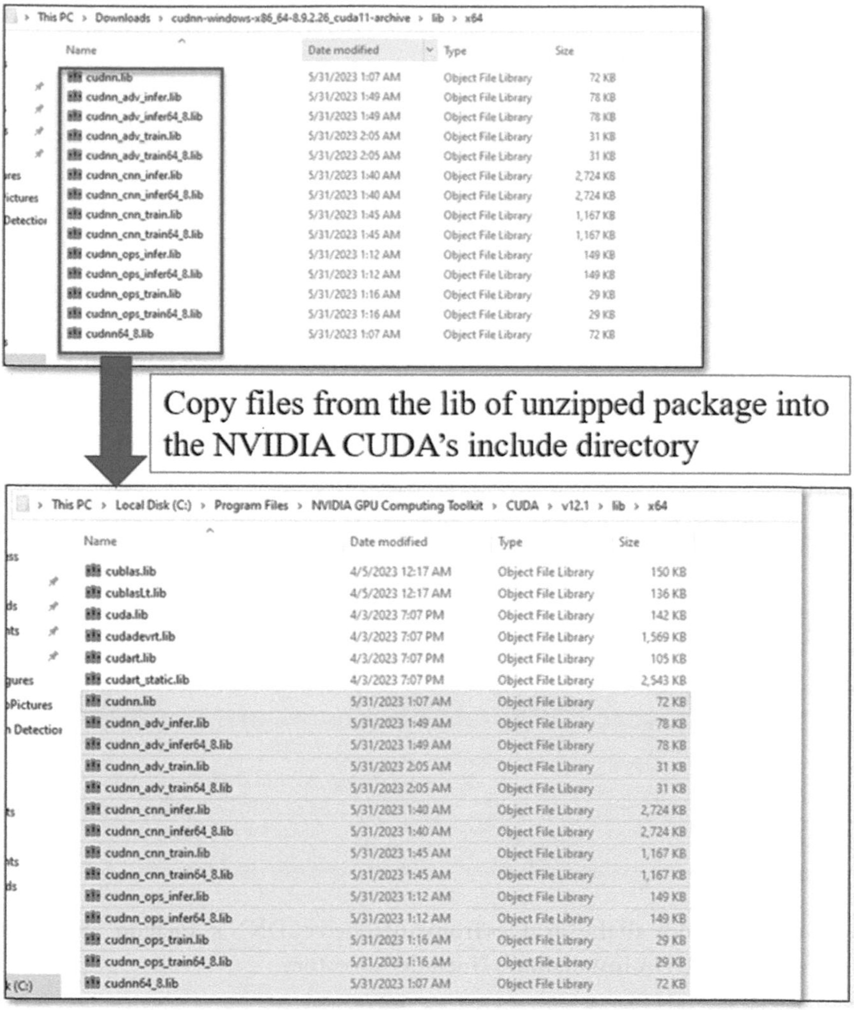

FIGURE 5.25 Copy all the ".lib" files from unzipped cuDNN's "...\lib\x64" and paste those into the CUDA installation's "...\lib\x64" directory.

cuDNN zip file names and CUDA versions based on Nvidia's recent release and updates.

Finally, add the location of "bin" (C:\Program Files\NVIDIA GPU Computing Toolkit\CUDA\v12.1\bin) to the Path of the system's environment variables. If you have the "libnvvp" directory inside the CUDA installation folder, which is a performance profiling tool for visual profilers'

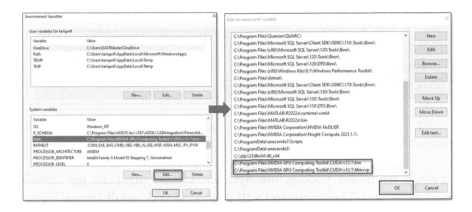

FIGURE 5.26   Update the system's environment variables Path and add the locations of "…\v12.1\bin" and "…\v12.1\libnvvp".

feedback on CUDA C/C++ applications, add that location to the Path, too (Figure 5.26). To edit and add these new paths to the system variables, follow the procedure shown in Figures 5.4 and 5.5.

5.5 SETUP OPENCV AND ADDITIONAL LIBRARIES

OpenCV (Open Source Computer Vision) is a computer vision library that is frequently used for image or video data manipulation during machine learning and deep learning applications. As of now, it has more than 2500 optimized algorithms, including numerous state-of-the-art algorithms for object detection or recognition, object tracking and image processing, image transformations, video analysis, and many more [19, 20]. It is considered the de-facto tool for a great number of engineers and researchers as it has leading contributions in the field of vision-sensing robots, autonomous cars, unmanned aerial vehicles, etc. In this book, for demonstrating the case studies, the OpenCV library is utilized.

To install OpenCV, open "Command Prompt" from the Windows search menu and launch it as administrator. The "Command Prompt" terminal typically runs from the user's profile (e.g., C:\Users\username), however, it will run from the "system32" directory of Windows if opened as administrator (e.g., C:\WINDOWS\system32). From the "system32" directory, change the directory location to the "Scripts" folder of the Anaconda installation using the command "cd" and "Scripts" folder location (Figure 5.27). (e.g., cd C:\ProgramData\anaconda3\Scripts). Then install

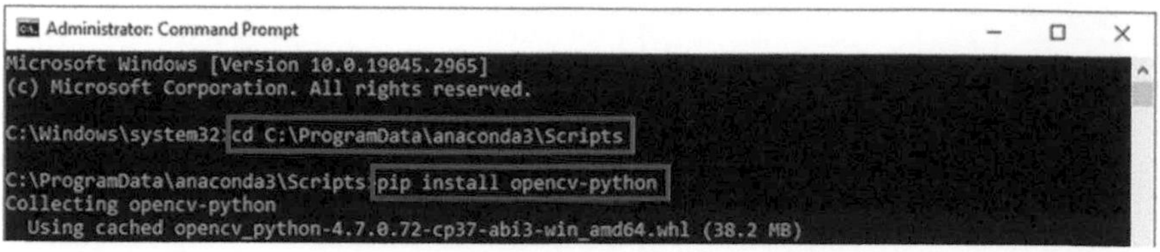

FIGURE 5.27   Install OpenCV using pip from the "Scripts" folder of Anaconda installation.

OpenCV using the package-management system pip (e.g., pip install opencv-python). This command will download and install OpenCV and related packages. Some of the packages that have already been installed by Anaconda installation or by any other previous Python package installations will return "Requirement already satisfied" notifications.

Next, install the image augmentation library called, "imgaug" [21]. This library is highly useful in deep learning applications as it can increase the number of training images artificially by applying various image processing and augmentation techniques. To install this library using pip, enter the command "pip install imgaug" in "Command Prompt" launched as administrator. Also, make sure that this command is entered from the "Scripts" folder of Anaconda, as shown in Figure 5.28.

PyTorch's "pretrainedmodels" need to be installed to access pre-trained convolutional networks with unique interfaces or APIs [22]. Although the "torchvision" library already has built-in model architectures with weights for various datasets, "pretrainedmodels" provide additional models to contribute to the PyTorch ecosystem. It can be installed by entering the command "pip install pretrainedmodels" from "Command Prompt" as administrator (Figure 5.29).

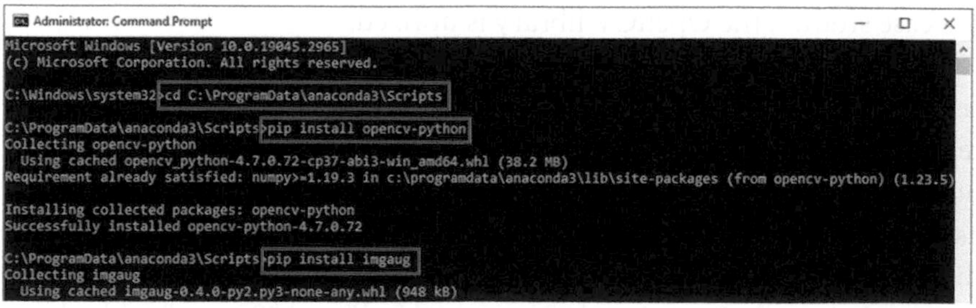

FIGURE 5.28   Install the image augmentation library using pip from the "Scripts" folder of the Anaconda installation.

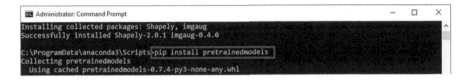

FIGURE 5.29   Install the "pretrainedmodels" using pip from the "Scripts" folder of Anaconda installation.

5.6 VERIFY CUDA SETUP

At this point, all the necessary libraries and packages are installed for training a deep learning model. All of the case studies of this book are done on a 64-bit Windows 10 Enterprise workstation with Intel(R) Core(TM) i9-10920X @ 2 × 3.50 GHz processor, 192 GB RAM, and two Nvidia GeForce RTX 3090 GPU workstation. In one case study, for demonstration purposes, the program was modified to run on a single GPU workstation. The configuration of the one GPU workstation is a 64-bit Windows 10 Enterprise workstation with Intel(R) Core(TM) i7-8700 @ 2 × 3.20 GHz processor, 32 GB RAM, and one Nvidia Quadro P1000 GPU. In the "Command Prompt" or "Anaconda Prompt" if we enter the command "nvidia-smi" it will return the GPU driver information (Figure 5.30).

If we want to verify if the GPUs are found by PyTorch or not, we can import "torch" in Spyder's console and use the command "torch.cuda.is_available()" similar to Figure 5.14. This time it will return True, and we can

```
 Anaconda Prompt

(base) C:\Users\tariqarif>nvidia-smi
Tue Jun  6 18:59:14 2023
+-----------------------------------------------------------------------------+
| NVIDIA-SMI 531.79       Driver Version: 531.79       CUDA Version: 12.1     |
|-------------------------------+----------------------+----------------------+
| GPU  Name            TCC/WDDM | Bus-Id        Disp.A | Volatile Uncorr. ECC |
| Fan  Temp  Perf  Pwr:Usage/Cap|         Memory-Usage | GPU-Util  Compute M. |
|                               |                      |               MIG M. |
|===============================+======================+======================|
|   0  NVIDIA GeForce RTX 3090    WDDM | 00000000:17:00.0 Off |                  N/A |
| 0%   52C    P8     35W / 420W|   8367MiB / 24576MiB |      1%      Default |
|                               |                      |                  N/A |
+-------------------------------+----------------------+----------------------+
|   1  NVIDIA GeForce RTX 3090    WDDM | 00000000:65:00.0  On |                  N/A |
| 0%   52C    P8     47W / 420W|   8367MiB / 24576MiB |      1%      Default |
|                               |                      |                  N/A |
+-------------------------------+----------------------+----------------------+
```

FIGURE 5.30   Use the "nvidia-smi" command in the "Command Prompt" or in the "Anaconda Prompt" to verify the graphics card information.

```
In [1]: import torch

In [2]: torch.cuda.is_available()
Out[2]: True

In [3]: torch.cuda.current_device()
Out[3]: 0

In [4]: torch.cuda.device_count()
Out[4]: 2

In [5]: torch.cuda.get_device_name(0)
Out[5]: 'NVIDIA GeForce RTX 3090'

In [6]: torch.cuda.get_device_name(1)
Out[6]: 'NVIDIA GeForce RTX 3090'
```

FIGURE 5.31   Verify if CUDA is found by PyTorch or not. Also, check the current CUDA device, number of CUDA devices, and device names.

check the current CUDA device, number of CUDA devices, and device names using the commands shown in Figure 5.31.

Although PyTorch is functional on a CPU, most of the engineering and tensor computations require the support of a GPU to process large datasets. This chapter is focused on the setup of Nvidia GPU and its computing toolkit CUDA to demonstrate computationally intensive deep learning training (Chapters 6–9) in practical settings.

REFERENCES

1. Abadi, M., Barham, P., Chen, J., Chen, Z., Davis, A., Dean, J., Devin, M., Ghemawat, S., Irving, G., Isard, M., Kudlur, M., Levenberg, J., Monga, R., Moore, S., Murray, D. G., Steiner, B., Tucker, P., Vasudevan, V., Warden, P., Wicke, M., Yu, Y., and Zheng, X., 2016, "TensorFlow: A System for Large-Scale Machine Learning," Proceedings of the 12th USENIX conference on Operating Systems Design and Implementation, USENIX Association, pp. 265–283.
2. Paszke, A., Gross, S., Massa, F., Lerer, A., Bradbury, J., Chanan, G., Killeen, T., Lin, Z., Gimelshein, N., Antiga, L., Desmaison, A., Köpf, A., Yang, E., DeVito, Z., Raison, M., Tejani, A., Chilamkurthy, S., Steiner, B., Fang, L., Bai, J., and Chintala, S., 2019, "PyTorch: An Imperative Style, High-Performance Deep Learning Library," Proceedings of the 33rd International Conference on Neural Information Processing Systems, Curran Associates Inc., p. 721.

3. Chollet, F., & others., 2015, "Keras: Deep Learning for humans," https://github.com.

4. Jia, Y., Shelhamer, E., Donahue, J., Karayev, S., Long, J., Girshick, R., Guadarrama, S., and Darrell, T., 2014, "Caffe: Convolutional Architecture for Fast Feature Embedding," Proceedings of the 22nd ACM International Conference on Multimedia, Association for Computing Machinery, pp. 675–678.

5. Seide, F., and Agarwal, A., 2016, "CNTK: Microsoft's Open-Source Deep-Learning Toolkit," Proceedings of the 22nd ACM SIGKDD International Conference on Knowledge Discovery and Data Mining, Association for Computing Machinery, p. 2135.

6. Team, T., Al-Rfou, R., Alain, G., Almahairi, A., Angermueller, C., Bahdanau, D., Ballas, N., Bastien, F., Bayer, J., Belikov, A., Belopolsky, A., Bengio, Y., Bergeron, A., Bergstra, J., Bisson, V., Bleecher Snyder, J., Bouchard, N., Boulanger-Lewandowski, N., Bouthillier, X., and Zhang, Y., 2016, "Theano: A Python framework for fast computation of mathematical expressions." https://arxiv.org/abs/1605.02688.

7. Gibson, A., Nicholson, C., Patterson, J., Warrick, M., Black, A., Kokorin, V., Audet, S., and Eraly, S., 2016, Deeplearning4j: Distributed, open-source deep learning for Java and Scala on Hadoop and Spark. https://figshare.com/articles/software/deeplearning4j-deeplearning4j-parent-0_4-rc3_8_zip/3362644/2.

8. 2020, "TensorFlow-based neural network library," https://github.com/deepmind/sonnet.

9. Tokui, S., Okuta, R., Akiba, T., Niitani, Y., Ogawa, T., Saito, S., Suzuki, S., Uenishi, K., Vogel, B., and Vincent, H. Y., 2019, "Chainer: A Deep Learning Framework for Accelerating the Research Cycle," Proceedings of the 25th ACM SIGKDD International Conference on Knowledge Discovery & Data Mining, Association for Computing Machinery, pp. 2002–2011.

10. Chen, T., Li, M., Li, Y., Lin, M., Wang, N., Wang, M., Xiao, T., Xu, B., Zhang, C., and Zhang, Z., 2015, "MXNet: A Flexible and Efficient Machine Learning Library for Heterogeneous Distributed Systems," https://arxiv.org/abs/1512.01274.

11. Dathathri, R., Gill, G., Hoang, L., Dang, H.-V., Brooks, A., Dryden, N., Snir, M., and Pingali, K., 2018, "Gluon: A Communication-Optimizing Substrate for Distributed Heterogeneous Graph Analytics," Proceedings of the 39th ACM SIGPLAN Conference on Programming Language Design and Implementation, Association for Computing Machinery, pp. 752–768.

12. NVIDIA Corporation, 2023, "Your GPU Compute Capability," https://developer.nvidia.com/cuda-gpus.

13. 2023, "GET STARTED - Select preferences and run the command to install PyTorch locally, or get started quickly with one of the supported cloud platforms," https://pytorch.org/get-started/locally/.

14. VS Revo Group Ltd., 2023, "Revo Uninstaller," https://www.revouninstaller.com/revo-uninstaller-free-download/.

15. NVIDIA Corporation, 2023, "NVIDIA cuDNN," https://developer.nvidia.com/cudnn.

16. 2023, "cuDNN Support Matrix," https://docs.nvidia.com/deeplearning/cudnn/support-matrix/index.html.

17. 2023, "CUDA Installation Guide for Microsoft Windows," https://docs.nvidia.com/cuda/cuda-installation-guide-microsoft-windows/index.html.

18. 2023, "NVIDIA cuDNN," https://developer.nvidia.com/cudnn.

19. Bradski, G., 2000, "The OpenCV Library," https://opencv.org/

20. 2023, "OpenCV," https://opencv.org/about/.

21. Jung, A., & others, 2020, "imgaug," https://github.com/aleju/imgaug.

22. Cadène, R., 2020, "Pretrained models for PyTorch," https://github.com/Cadene/pretrained-models.pytorch.

## CHAPTER 6

Case Study I

Image Classification

6.1 PROBLEM STATEMENT

This case study demonstrates a practical implementation of deep learning for image classification problems. Here, we have used transfer learning to leverage the benefit of feature extractions using a pre-trained model. To train and test our model, an open-source dataset containing 877 images of traffic signs that are divided into four classes (Traffic light, Stop, Speed limit, and Crosswalk) is used. The dataset is available on Kaggle's site and can be downloaded from [1]. The program structure presented in this case study and other case studies of this book maintains a similar coding structure for ease of understanding.

The "Road Sign Detection" data provides rectangular bounding box dimensions for every image as Pascal Virtual Object Classes (VOC) XML annotations that are found in the download folder titled "annotations". There are 877 annotated XML files (road0.xml to road876.xml) in the "annotations" folder to label 877 road images (road0.png to road876.png) in the "image" folder. The goal of Case Study I is to train a deep learning model using the given images with labels and evaluate the trained model using unknown or unseen traffic signs. If trained properly, the model should classify any image in one of the four categories: traffic light, stop, speed limit, and crosswalk. We recommend readers of this book download the dataset and reproduce the results by following the instructions given in Chapter 5 and executing the codes given in this chapter.

DOI: 10.1201/9781003402923-6

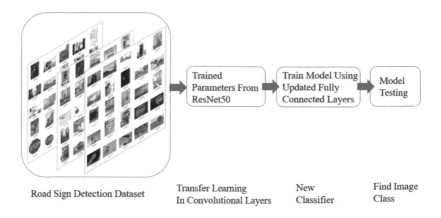

Road Sign Detection Dataset   Transfer Learning In Convolutional Layers   New Classifier   Find Image Class

FIGURE 6.1 Schematic of transfer learning using a pre-trained deep learning network, ResNet50.

To identify the different classes of images, the pre-trained model "ResNet50" was used [2]. The "ResNet50" is a popular variation of the residual network (ResNet) architecture that is primarily used for image classification tasks. It has fifty hidden layers and is trained on the ImageNet dataset. ResNet architectures are efficient in addressing the vanishing gradient problem during backpropagation. For this reason, ResNet and its variations are widely used as a starting point of transfer learning in image classification when large datasets with labels are available. A schematic of the transfer learning process using the pre-trained network is shown in Figure 6.1. After successful training and testing on the data set, we have used several random road sign pictures (downloaded from online) to evaluate the performance of the deep learning model on unseen images.

In the following sections, Python codes for the training and testing operations are explained. All of the codes presented in this chapter are written and executed using Spyder Integrated Developed Environment (IDE) from Anaconda. It is important to note that Spyder IDE should be opened using Anaconda Navigator or by executing the "spyder" command in "Anaconda Prompt". Otherwise, the program may not find the required CUDA environment for PyTorch, and the "torch.cuda.is_available()" command in Spyder's console will return "False".

6.2 DEFINING DEFAULT CONFIGURATION

In a large Python programming task, it is convenient to create Python classes that can group similar types of data and functions. The "Class" in Python forms an object to maintain a set of attributes. Here, in this

```
class DefaultConfigs(object):
    Image_PATH = r"C:\Users\tariqarif\Desktop\Road Sign Detection\archive\images"
    Annot_PATH = r"C:\Users\tariqarif\Desktop\Road Sign Detection\archive\annotations"
    Model_PATH = r"C:\Users\tariqarif\Desktop\Road Sign Detection\archive"
    num_classes = 4
    img_width = 256
    img_height = 256
    channels = 3
    lr = 0.001
    batch_size = 128
    epochs = 20
    seed= 112

config = DefaultConfigs()
```

FIGURE 6.2 Create a "DefaultConfigs" class to define parameters that will be used throughout the program.

program, a new class variable (DefaultConfigs) is created to set or define important default parameters (objects) that can be used throughout the program. The "DefaultConfigs" class is called using the "config" variable (Figure 6.2), and all of the class attributes can be accessed using the reference operator dot, ".". Here, declared class objects are "Image_PATH", "Annot_PATH", and "Model_PATH" to assign data locations and save model parameters in that path. The "num_classes", "img_width", "img_height", "channels", "lr" (learning rate), "batch_size", "epochs", and, "seed" are defined to assign default numerical values.

6.3 RANDOM SEED AND IMPORT MODULES/LIBRARIES

In this section, major modules and libraries required for running deep learning are presented. The "random", "numpy", and "troch" libraries are imported, and all random seeds are set using the "seed" value assigned in default configurations. The "torch" is required for using PyTorch's framework with deep learning models [3], the "numpy" library is for manipulating multi-dimensional arrays, and the seed number is used to assign reproducibility to the program where any values can be chosen arbitrarily. A function "set_all_random_seed" is defined to set random seeds of "numpy" and "torch" using the default seed assigned in Figure 6.2. Figure 6.3 shows the commands in Spyder editor for importing these libraries and the function.

Next, Python's "os" module to interact with the operating system, "minidom" from "xml.dom" for accessing XML documents, and "pandas" library for data analysis and manipulations are imported. Figure 6.3 shows the commands in Spyder editor for importing these modules and libraries.

Next, the variable "annotations" is created to define the location of the "annotations" folder in the operating system, and the list of all files and directories inside "annotations" are accessed using the pandas data

```
########################
#import libraries and set random seeds
import random
import numpy as np
import torch

def set_all_random_seed(seed = config.seed):
    random.seed(seed)
    np.random.seed(seed)
    torch.manual_seed(seed)
    torch.cuda.manual_seed_all(seed)
    return seed

print(f'random seed {set_all_random_seed()}')

########################
#import librarie and read in data and create dataframe
import os                        # to list all files in a folder
from xml.dom import minidom      #to process the XML documents
import pandas as pd              #to create dataframe object
```

FIGURE 6.3 Import random, numpy, torch, operating system module, minidom, pandas modules, and a function for setting random seed.

frame. All the. xml files (road0.xml to road876.xml) in "annotations" are parsed iteratively using a for loop and XML data for image "label" and bounding box dimensions ("xmin", "xmax", "ymin", and "ymax") are accessed. These data are appended inside a list called "all_data_list". For example, the XML file "road1.xml" has the root tag "<annotation>" and under this tag, it has different child tags such as "<folder>", "<filename", "<size>", etc. (Figure 6.4). For our analysis, the required data needed to be parsed from XML files are filename, name (or label), xmin, ymin, xmax, and ymax.

Figure 6.4 shows the "road1.xml" file information in a text file, and Figure 6.5 shows the parsing or extracting of yellow highlighted "tagged" information (Figure 6.4) from each XML file iteratively using a for loop.

Extracted data from XML files are assigned to "all_data" using the panda data frame, and column headers are created. After executing all commands up to Figure 6.5, if we print "all_data" in Spyder IDE, it will display the data frame in a tabular format as shown in Figure 6.6.

After storing the data in "all_data", a label encoder is used to evaluate categorical columns using numerical values, and the "fit_transform" method from the "sklearn. preprocessing" class is used to pre-process

```
<annotation>
    <folder>images</folder>
    <filename>road1.png</filename>
    <size>
        <width>400</width>
        <height>283</height>
        <depth>3</depth>
    </size>
    <segmented>0</segmented>
    <object>
        <name>trafficlight</name>
        <pose>Unspecified</pose>
        <truncated>0</truncated>
        <occluded>0</occluded>
        <difficult>0</difficult>
        <bndbox>
            <xmin>154</xmin>
            <ymin>63</ymin>
            <xmax>258</xmax>
            <ymax>281</ymax>
        </bndbox>
    </object>
</annotation>
```

FIGURE 6.4 Information in the "road1.xml" file after opening as a text.

data for training. The "fit_transform" method helps to converge the solution in the training process and minimizes the problem of over-shooting the minima [4]. An additional dictionary with mapping is created to get the labels assigned from "0" to "3". Also, all data were randomly divided into training and testing datasets using the "train_test_split()" method.

```
annotations = os.listdir(config.Annot_PATH)
all_data_list = []
for annots in annotations:
    file = minidom.parse(config.Annot_PATH+'/'+annots)
    filename = file.getElementsByTagName('filename')[0].firstChild.data
    label = file.getElementsByTagName('name')[0].firstChild.data
    xmin = file.getElementsByTagName('xmin')[0].firstChild.data
    ymin = file.getElementsByTagName('ymin')[0].firstChild.data
    xmax = file.getElementsByTagName('xmax')[0].firstChild.data
    ymax = file.getElementsByTagName('ymax')[0].firstChild.data
    all_data_list.append([filename,label,xmin,ymin,xmax,ymax])

all_data = pd.DataFrame(all_data_list)
all_data.columns = ['filename','label','xmin','ymin','xmax','ymax']
```

FIGURE 6.5 Iterative parsing operation to fetch required data from every XML file.

```
In [2]: print(all_data)
          filename          label xmin ymin xmax ymax
0          road0.png  trafficlight   98   62  208  232
1          road1.png  trafficlight  154   63  258  281
2         road10.png  trafficlight  106    3  244  263
3        road100.png    speedlimit   35    5  363  326
4        road101.png    speedlimit  195    7  392  194
..            ...           ...    ...  ...  ...  ...
872       road95.png          stop   90  101  268  257
873       road96.png          stop  209   58  326  179
874       road97.png          stop   42   66  130  154
875       road98.png          stop  138   17  376  245
876       road99.png          stop   41   35  222  214

[877 rows x 6 columns]
```

FIGURE 6.6   Print "all_data" that displays tabular data (in Spyder's console) collected from XML files for every image.

Figure 6.7 shows this data split where the test data size is 20% of the total data. An integer (config.seed) 112 was assigned to "random_state" so that the code could reproduce identical outputs later.

Next, we import the OpenCV library for computer vision operations [5], "torch" for using PyTorch's framework with deep learning models [3], "Dataset" library for maintaining the data set effectively during the training process [3], "transform" for transforming images [6], open cv for reading image files, and "augmenters" for implementing image augmentation sequences such as crop, horizontal/vertical flips, pooling, and gaussian blurs [7]. The commands for importing these libraries and modules are shown in Figure 6.8.

```
############################
# process labels
from sklearn import preprocessing

le = preprocessing.LabelEncoder()
all_data['label1'] = le.fit_transform(all_data.label)
le_name_mapping = dict(zip(le.transform(le.classes_),le.classes_))

############################
#split the dataset into train and validation sets
from sklearn.model_selection import train_test_split

train_data_list,valid_data_list = train_test_split(all_data,test_size = 0.20,
                                          random_state = config.seed)
```

FIGURE 6.7   Use the "fit_transfrom()" method to pre-process data, create a dictionary to check the labels, and split data randomly for training and validation.

```
#############################
#prepare the dataset
from torch.utils.data import Dataset
from torchvision import transforms as T    # to transform the data into a tensor and normalize it
import cv2                                   # to read image files and process
from imgaug import augmenters as iaa         # to perform image augmentation
```

FIGURE 6.8   Import "Dataset", "transforms", "cv2", and "augmenters" modules and libraries.

6.4 DEFINE DATASET CLASS AND ATTRIBUTES

A new class variable called "TrafficDataset" is defined that has four different attributes. These are "images_df", "augment", "mode", "mean", and "std". These attribute assignments are shown in Figure 6.9. The "__init__" method is used for setting up the initial value of the instance, the "__len__" method returns the number of image items in the "images_df", and the "__getitem__" method read images using indices and creates labels for training. The "augmentor()" method is utilized by "__getitem__" to aid the artificial image generations. It also uses "ToTensor()" to convert the "ndarray" (image features) to tensors and scale pixel intensity values from 0 to 1 [8].

Inside the "TrafficDataset" class, a method called "read_images" is created to read and crop images using the bounding box dimensions given with the dataset. The cropped image data type is then converted to unsigned "uint8" format (0–255) and resized into default image weight/height as defined by default configurations (Figure 6.10).

```
class TrafficDataset(Dataset):
    def __init__(self,images_df,base_path,mean,std,augment=True,mode="train"):
        self.images_df = images_df.copy()
        self.augment = augment
        self.mode = mode
        self.mean = mean
        self.std = std

    def __len__(self):
        return len(self.images_df)

    def __getitem__(self,index):
        X = self.read_images(index)

        if not self.mode == "test":
            y = self.images_df.iloc[index].label1

        else:
            y = (self.images_df.iloc[index].filename)

        if self.augment:
            X = self.augmentor(X)

        X = T.Compose([T.ToTensor(),T.Normalize(self.mean,self.std)])(X.copy())#please pass a copy of the X here
        return X.float(),y                      # convert the image to floatTensor, as model weights are in floatTensor
```

FIGURE 6.9   The "TrafficDataset" class and "__init__", "__len__", "__getitem__" methods.

```
def read_images(self,index):
    row = self.images_df.iloc[index]
    filename = str(config.Image_PATH + '/' + row.filename)
    image = cv2.imread(filename)

    xmin = int(row.xmin)
    ymin = int(row.ymin)
    xmax = int(row.xmax)
    ymax = int(row.ymax)

    cropped_image = np.array(image[ymin:ymax, xmin:xmax])
    images = cropped_image/255.0                        #normalize the image

    return cv2.resize(images,(config.img_width,config.img_height))
```

FIGURE 6.10 "read_image" method to crop using bounding box dimensions, change data types to "unit8", and resize images.

```
def augmentor(self,image):
    seq = iaa.Sequential([
        iaa.OneOf([
            iaa.Affine(rotate=90),
            iaa.Affine(rotate=180),
            iaa.Affine(rotate=270),
            iaa.Affine(shear=(-16, 16)),
            iaa.Fliplr(0.5),

        ])], random_order=True)

    image_aug = seq.augment_image(image)
    return image_aug
```

FIGURE 6.11 "Augmentor" method for applying one of the operations randomly: rotate the image 90 degrees, 180 degrees, 270 degrees, apply shear and flip operations.

In order to increase the number of training images, an image augmentation technique is applied. The image augmentation method typically improves the model performance as it increases the original number of images available in the dataset. We have used an "augmentor" method to rotate images 90, 180, and 270 degrees, shear images by −16 to 16 degrees, and apply flip operations to 50% of images. These operations are done in random order (one of the operations is selected randomly each time) by setting the "random_order" to "True" as shown in Figure 6.11.

6.5 LOAD DATASET AND MODEL ARCHITECTURE

To normalize the model, we need to use mean and standard deviations corresponding to the deep learning architecture. For ResNet50, the mean is [0.485, 0.456, 0.406], and std is [0.229, 0.224, 0.225] [9]. We import

```
# use the appropriate mean and std values that the model expects
mean=[0.485, 0.456, 0.406]
std=[0.229, 0.224, 0.225]

train_gen = TrafficDataset(train_data_list,config.Image_PATH,mean,std,augment=True,mode="train")
val_gen = TrafficDataset(valid_data_list,config.Image_PATH,mean,std,augment=False,mode="eval")

#########################
#create dataloader object to iterate over the datasets
from torch.utils.data import DataLoader

train_loader = DataLoader(train_gen,batch_size=config.batch_size,shuffle=True,pin_memory=True)
val_loader = DataLoader(val_gen,batch_size=config.batch_size,shuffle=False,pin_memory=True)
```

FIGURE 6.12   "DataLoader" constructor to facilitate easy access for training and validation datasets.

"DataLoader" from the torch utility [3]. The data loading utility of PyTorch (DataLoader), is used with arguments for dataset ("train_gen"), batch size, shuffling, and pin memory. This constructor wraps an iterable around the defined dataset ("train_gen" or "val_gen") and facilitates easy access to the images. Detailed explanations of these arguments are found in [10]. The validation testing is also done using the "DataLoader" but on the validation dataset without shuffling (Figure 6.12).

After the data set is imported and pre-processed, the next step would be importing a trained deep learning network and adjusting its input/output parameters to match with the classification problem. At this stage, we also need to import packages required to run a convolutional network.

The "nn" and "optim" modules of PyTorch are imported. The "nn" module is used for training neural networks, and the "optim" module can be used to implement different optimization algorithms that are available in PyTorch [11, 12]. The pre-trained model "resnet50" and its weights are imported from the "torchvision.models" module. "torchvision" provides many popular pre-trained models such as AlexNet, VGG, ResNets, SqueezeNet, Inception V3, GoogLeNet, MobileNet v2, etc. These models can be used directly for inference or transfer learning. If the model fails to load and shows a certificate issue, we need to import an "ssl" certificate to create a default context so that the code secures the default settings (Figure 6.13).

After loading the "resnet50" model with default parameters, its input dimension of the fully connected layers is checked (input_dim=2048). Also, the default number of output features of the fully connected layers is 1000. Therefore, it is required to change these parameters in the last linear layers so that it match our classification problem which has four output classes (config.num_classes=4). The sequential network architecture is applied by using "nn.Sequential" from PyTorch so that the layers

```
# define the  pretrained model for tranfer learning
from torch import nn,optim
from torchvision.models import resnet50, ResNet50_Weights
                # may use any other models for image classifications

#run if downloading model failed. model certificate issue
import ssl
ssl._create_default_https_context = ssl._create_unverified_context

model = resnet50(weights=ResNet50_Weights.DEFAULT)
input_dim = model.fc.in_features
model.fc = nn.Sequential(                    #check the model and change the last
        nn.BatchNorm1d(input_dim),      #linear layer to output number of classes of the dataset
        nn.Dropout(0.5),
        nn.Linear(input_dim, config.num_classes)
    )
```

FIGURE 6.13   Importing pre-trained model and updating fully connected layers using "nn.sequential".

are sequentially used one after another, as shown in Figure 6.13. In the forward sequence of the model network, we have used the dropout regularization method where 50% ("nn.dropout") of nodes are randomly dropped to avoid overfitting training data. The "nn.Linear" changes the input and output features of the imported model to match the dataset and to determine the final class from model prediction.

If we want to load a pre-trained model from "pretrainedmodels.model" module (e.g., bninception), it may not be found by the program and will return an error saying "No module named pretrained models". In that situation, we will need to install pre-trained models using the command "pip install pretrained models" (Figure 6.14). This installation needs to be done in the "Anaconda Prompt" so that the settings will remain in Spyder when run from Anaconda. Once installed, the program will be able to load the model without any error.

Also, it is recommended to run Spyder IDE (every time) from "Anacoda Prompt" by entering the command "spyder" and running each of the program sections separately. For example, to run a section of the program in Spyder IDE (Windows), we may select multiple lines of code and press the "F9" button. This process will help the user to understand the codes step-by-step and pinpoint an error quickly.

```
(base) C:\Users\tariqarif>pip install pretrainedmodels
Collecting pretrainedmodels
  Downloading pretrainedmodels-0.7.4.tar.gz (58 kB)
  ---------------------------------------- 58.8/58.8 kB 1.6 MB/s eta 0:00:00
```

FIGURE 6.14   Installing pre-trained models from "Anaconda Prompt".

6.6 TRAINING SETUP FOR MULTI-GPU WORKSTATION

The workstation used for data training, and testing might have one or multiple Graphical Processing Units (GPUs). In this section, we present the Python codes that are used for multiple (two or more) GPUs. The workstation we used has two Nvidia GPUs (GeForce RTX 3090 × 2). Since we want to utilize both of the GPUs for distributed training tasks, "nn. DataParallel" is implemented on the model. This data parallel operation splits the batches and trains independently in all available GPUs. For the effective parallel calculations on Nvidia GPUs, the CUDA platform ("model.cuda()") is used (Figure 6.15).

The Pytorch's "optim" package is utilized for accessing various built-in optimization algorithms. In this example, we have implemented a stochastic gradient descent (SGD) algorithm with a momentum factor of 0.9 and weight decay 1e-4. The momentum and weight decay are optional parameters that minimize the impact of noises in convergence and improve the generalization performance of the model [13, 14].

We then use the cross-entropy loss (nn.CrossEntropyLoss()) criterion, which measures the difference between the predicted probability distribution and the ground truth distribution. The step learning rate schedulers with a step size of 5 and multiplicative factor of learning rate decay, 0.3 are implemented to reduce the learning rate during the training process. Finally, the "requires_grad" is set to True for instructing automatic differentiation or "autograd" recording operation. The codes for the parallel operation, SGD optimization, loss function, and automatic gradient recording are shown in Figure 6.15. In some deep learning problems, it is beneficial to freeze the model (set param.requires_grad = False) and run for five or ten epochs, and then unfreeze the model (set param.requires_grad = True) and run the remaining 15 or 20 epochs. This trick may help

```
model = nn.DataParallel(model) # use this for multiple GPU
model= model.cuda()

#define loss function, optimizer, and scheduler
criterion = nn.CrossEntropyLoss().cuda()
optimizer = optim.SGD(model.parameters(),lr = config.lr,momentum=0.9,weight_decay=1e-4)

scheduler = optim.lr_scheduler.StepLR(optimizer,step_size=5,gamma=0.3)

## you can manually freeze ot unfreeze the weights of a model. To freeze the model set
## param.requires_grad = False
for param in model.parameters():
    param.requires_grad = True
```

FIGURE 6.15   Using parallel Nvidia GPUs, define a loss function, optimizer, and schedule learning rate.

the model to achieve better accuracy. In this case study, the model weights were unfrozen all the time. But in the next chapter, for the object detection case study, this scenario is presented.

6.7 MODEL TRAINING AND SAVING THE BEST MODEL

The final stage is to train the model on the dataset and save model parameters that have minimum losses. Figure 6.16 shows the code for training the model on CUDA using forward and back propagation and calculating loss in every iteration. A nested "for loop" is used to run the model for a number of epochs set by the default configurations ("config. epochs"). Initially, the best loss is set to a very large number (np.inf),

```
#Train the model
steps = 0
train_loss = 0
train_accuracy = 0
best_loss= np.inf

for epoch in range(config.epochs):
    model.train()
    scheduler.step(epoch)
    for images, labels in iter(train_loader):
        images, labels = images.cuda(), labels.type(torch.LongTensor).cuda() #LongTensor as the classes
                                                                              #will be integer
        optimizer.zero_grad()
        output = model.forward(images)
        loss = criterion(output, labels)
        loss.backward()
        optimizer.step()

        train_loss += loss.item()                                    #keep track of the losses

        #accuracy estimation
        ps = torch.exp(output)
        equality = (labels.data == ps.max(dim=1)[1])
        train_accuracy += equality.type(torch.FloatTensor).mean()
        steps += 1
        if steps % 10 == 0:
            model.eval()
            val_loss = 0
            val_accuracy = 0
            with torch.no_grad():
                for images, labels in iter(val_loader):
                    images, labels = images.cuda(), labels.type(torch.LongTensor).cuda()
                    output = model.forward(images)
                    val_loss += criterion(output, labels).item()
                    ps = torch.exp(output)
                    equality = (labels.data == ps.max(dim=1)[1])
                    val_accuracy += equality.type(torch.FloatTensor).mean()

                if val_loss/len(val_loader) < best_loss:             #keep track of the loss, and update if decrease
                    best_loss = val_loss/len(val_loader)
                    print('saving model...')
                    torch.save(model, config.Model_PATH+'/model.pt') #if val_loss decreases, save the model
            #print the losses and accuracies
            print("Epoch: {}/{}.. ".format(epoch+1, config.epochs),
                  "Training Loss: {:.3f}.. ".format(train_loss/10),
                  "Training Accuracy: {:.3f}".format(train_accuracy/10),
                  "Validation Loss: {:.3f}.. ".format(val_loss/len(val_loader)),
                  "Validation Accuracy: {:.3f}".format(val_accuracy/len(val_loader)))
            train_loss = 0
            train_accuracy = 0
            model.train()
print('Finish!')
```

FIGURE 6.16 Model training using forward and backward propagation, and determining the best model that has minimum validation loss.

and after every iteration, the program compares it with the previous best loss found.

As the for loop iterates over each batch of training images, it determines training losses and accuracies. For the validation, the model runs over the validation dataset, checks image labels, and compares them with the labels from the model output. If the model finds a minimum loss during validation, it saves the model parameters as the best model. The code in Figure 6.16 is used to train and find a model that has optimum weights, and stores the best model in a location assigned by "config.Model_PATH". During this process, the program also prints loss and accuracies for training and validation.

The model training may return the "OutOfMemoryError: CUDA out of memory" error, which is an issue of GPU memory limitations. In that situation, the code won't execute. We can resolve this memory problem by reducing the batch size (e.g., 128 to 64 or 32) or image height and width (e.g., 512 to 256).

6.8 TRAINING SETUP FOR SINGLE GPU WORKSTATION

The codes presented in Figures 6.2–6.16 need to be modified for a single GPU workstation. One modification is to uncomment or delete the code section that uses the data parallel module to split inputs across GPUs. So, the code in Figure 6.15 needs to be updated to Figure 6.17.

The model in one GPU system may return the "OutOfMemoryError: CUDA out of memory" error. In that case, the batch size in "DefaultConfigs" should be reduced. We tested this code using one GPU workstation (one Nvidia Quadro P1000 GPU), where the training doesn't execute due to a CUDA memory error. Once the batch size is reduced to 16, the program runs without any issues (Figure 6.18). Depending on GPU and transfer model,

```
#model = nn.DataParallel(model) # use this for multiple GPU
model= model.cuda()

#define loss function, optimizer, and scheduler
criterion = nn.CrossEntropyLoss().cuda()
optimizer = optim.SGD(model.parameters(),lr = config.lr,momentum=0.9,weight_decay=1e-4)

scheduler = optim.lr_scheduler.StepLR(optimizer,step_size=5,gamma=0.3)

## you can manually freeze ot unfreeze the weights of a model. To freeze the model set
## param.requires_grad = False
for param in model.parameters():
    param.requires_grad = True
```

FIGURE 6.17   Disable data parallelism for 1 GPU workstation.

```
class DefaultConfigs(object):
    Image_PATH = r"C:\Users\tariqarif\Desktop\Road Sign Detection\archive\images"
    Annot_PATH = r"C:\Users\tariqarif\Desktop\Road Sign Detection\archive\annotations"
    Model_PATH = r"C:\Users\tariqarif\Desktop\Road Sign Detection\archive"
    num_classes = 4
    img_width = 256
    img_height = 256
    channels = 3
    lr = 0.001
    batch_size = 16
    epochs = 20
    seed= 112

config = DefaultConfigs()
```

FIGURE 6.18   Reduce the batch size to 16 for resolving the "OutOfMemoryError: CUDA out of memory" error.

different batch sizes (e.g., 8, 16, 32, etc.) and image sizes (img_width and img_height) should be tested.

Once the model runs and starts to train, we will get the losses and accuracies printed for every few epochs. In this case study, the training and validation datasets are randomly split, where the allocated training and validation images are 80% and 20% of the total images, respectively. In some machine learning practices, the total dataset is divided into three different categories: training, validation, and testing. Although both validation and testing datasets can be used interchangeably for unbiased evaluation of the model, the validation dataset may be utilized for early stopping in overfitting scenarios [15]. After 20 epochs, we find the best minimum validation loss is 0.251, which yields a training accuracy of 93.9%, and a validation accuracy of 96.5% (Figure 6.19). In the first few epochs, if we find the training accuracies are increasing, but the validation accuracies are decreasing, the training should be terminated as it indicates that the model is failing to generalize the dataset and is overfitting.

```
Epoch: 7/20..  Training Loss: 0.422..  Training Accuracy: 0.887 Validation Loss: 0.424..  Validation Accuracy: 0.932
saving model...
Epoch: 9/20..  Training Loss: 0.309..  Training Accuracy: 0.926 Validation Loss: 0.334..  Validation Accuracy: 0.940
saving model...
Epoch: 10/20..  Training Loss: 0.307..  Training Accuracy: 0.929 Validation Loss: 0.292..  Validation Accuracy: 0.951
Epoch: 12/20..  Training Loss: 0.282..  Training Accuracy: 0.936 Validation Loss: 0.312..  Validation Accuracy: 0.936
Epoch: 14/20..  Training Loss: 0.293..  Training Accuracy: 0.941 Validation Loss: 0.335..  Validation Accuracy: 0.936
saving model...
Epoch: 15/20..  Training Loss: 0.288..  Training Accuracy: 0.945 Validation Loss: 0.278..  Validation Accuracy: 0.951
saving model...
Epoch: 17/20..  Training Loss: 0.269..  Training Accuracy: 0.939 Validation Loss: 0.251..  Validation Accuracy: 0.965
Epoch: 19/20..  Training Loss: 0.238..  Training Accuracy: 0.956 Validation Loss: 0.253..  Validation Accuracy: 0.965
Epoch: 20/20..  Training Loss: 0.241..  Training Accuracy: 0.950 Validation Loss: 0.262..  Validation Accuracy: 0.951
Finish!
```

FIGURE 6.19   "Training Accuracy" is 93.9% and "Validation Accuracy" is 96.5% for minimum validation loss.

6.9 MODEL TESTING AND INFERENCE

We may test the model performance by loading the best model from the model path (config.Model_PATH) and by classifying images from the dataset manually. Figures 6.20 and 6.21 show the code required to display an image from the "val_loader" batch, check the given label, and predict the label using the trained model. In the model classification, 0, 1, 2, and 3 refer to the labels, "Crosswalk", "Speed Limit", "Stop", and "Traffic Light", respectively. The code section in Figure 6.20 returns the features and labels tensor sizes in a batch and a label selected by the index number (label 0, i.e., crosswalk). The "pyplot" from the "matplotlib" library is used to plot the image defined by index 3, as shown in Figure 6.20.

Now we check the same image using the trained model. First, the model is set to the inference mode by using the "eval()" function so that the images in CUDA can be classified. The classification of the image in index 3 is printed using the code in Figure 6.21. It returns the output "Predicted Label: crosswalk".

For the inference, the model can also be tested by using random pictures in the context of real world. The images used for inference are not from the dataset and have different distributions. To test this, four

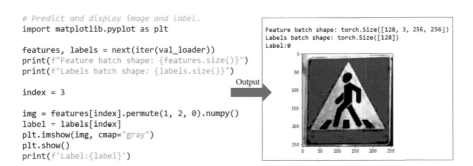

```
# Predict and display image and label.
import matplotlib.pyplot as plt

features, labels = next(iter(val_loader))
print(f"Feature batch shape: {features.size()}")
print(f"Labels batch shape: {labels.size()}")

index = 3

img = features[index].permute(1, 2, 0).numpy()
label = labels[index]
plt.imshow(img, cmap="gray")
plt.show()
print(f'Label:{label}')
```

Output →

```
Feature batch shape: torch.Size([128, 3, 256, 256])
Labels batch shape: torch.Size([128])
Label:0
```

FIGURE 6.20 Checking tensor sizes of features and labels, and displaying an image in index 3 and its label.

```
#Prediction by trained model
images = features.cuda()
output = model.forward(images)
pred_labels = np.argmax(output.cpu().detach().numpy(), axis=1)

print(f"Predicted Label: {le_name_mapping[pred_labels[index]]}")
```

FIGURE 6.21 Classify feature images from the validation dataset using the trained model and check the label for the image in index 3.

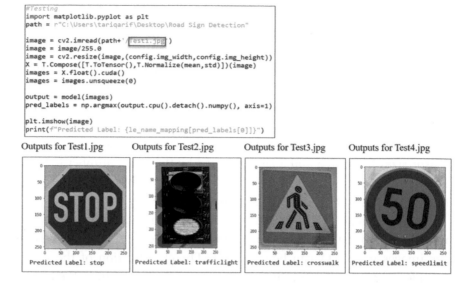

```
#Testing
import matplotlib.pyplot as plt
path = r"C:\Users\tariqarif\Desktop\Road Sign Detection"

image = cv2.imread(path+'/Test1.jpg')
image = image/255.0
image = cv2.resize(image,(config.img_width,config.img_height))
X = T.Compose([T.ToTensor(),T.Normalize(mean,std)])(image)
images = X.float().cuda()
images = images.unsqueeze(0)

output = model(images)
pred_labels = np.argmax(output.cpu().detach().numpy(), axis=1)

plt.imshow(image)
print(f"Predicted Label: {le_name_mapping[pred_labels[0]]}")
```

FIGURE 6.22   Model inference using road sign images that are outside of the dataset.

different open-source pictures are downloaded from https://unsplash. com/. These pictures are renamed (e.g., Test1.jpg, Test2.jpg, Test3.jpg, and Test4.jpg) and cropped for model evaluation (available in additional resources). The trained model can determine image classes successfully, as shown in Figure 6.22. The uncropped images are also available in the "UncroppedTestImage" folder. The model can also make correct predictions on uncropped images but with a lower accuracy rate. The program code is given in Figures 6.2–6.22 is available in the "main.py" of additional resources.

6.9.1 Fine Tuning

In deep learning, finding the optimal set of parameters for the best learning process is a challenge. It is always recommended to tweak different parameters and evaluate the outputs that minimize the loss function, increase accuracy, or reduce training/inference time. This process of finding the best set of combinations for optimal training is also called "Hyperparameter Tuning" (also discussed in Section 2.7.1). There is no definitive set of hyperparameters that should be tuned for a particular type of training operation. It can be changing the network architecture, such as the number of nodes, activation function, and layer types, or it can be utilizing different network objects, such as various optimizers and loss functions.

Hyperparameter tuning can also be done by modifying model training parameters such as batch size, learning rate, epoch numbers, etc. For example, the entire dataset can be passed in one batch to the GPU for training, but tuning batch size is efficient in terms of GPU memory allocations. A smaller batch size will minimize the GPU utilization, but it will increase the number of iterations. In many cases, a smaller batch size may show more training stability compared to a larger batch size. Typically, using an initial batch size of 32 is considered good practice for image datasets. The batch size can then be modified (e.g., 64, 128, etc.) to observe changes in the model performance. To improve the training speed, the number of epochs can be modified. A low number of epochs can be used for stability and need less training time compared to a high number of epochs, but it also tends to reduce model performance. Although high epoch numbers are better for model performance, after a certain value, it doesn't affect the training at all. A high epoch number can also trigger model instability.

The number of hidden layers and nodes used in each layer is also very critical and can be tuned for a better training process. Finding an optimum number of hidden layers can be a challenge as the training/inference time increases exponentially with the number of layers and nodes. Also, for a small and simple dataset, if too many hidden layers and nodes are used, the model can overfit. However, for learning from highly complex and unpredictable data, a high number of hidden layers or nodes can be useful. Therefore, determining an optimum combination of hyperparameters is a matter of trial and error and should be evaluated with intuition by considering data types and computational power. If enough time is available, it is preferred to search for an optimum set of parameters in a specific range using grid search. Hyperparameters can also be searched and tuned randomly in conjunction with an individual's experience and intuitions.

Now, let us explore some effects of hyperparameters over the training process. To demonstrate the effect of batch size, in this case, study, we present the training and validation results found by different batch sizes. These tests are done on the multi-GPU workstation (2×Nvidia RTX 3090 GPU). A batch size of 64 (batch_size = 64 in DefaultConfigs) shows improved training accuracy compared to a batch size of 128. We find the training accuracy is 98.7%, and the validation accuracy is 99.3% after 20 epochs, as shown in Figure 6.23. It should be noted that this example is using a multi-GPU workstation, and for a single GPU workstation, these accuracies are likely to change.

```
Epoch: 14/20..  Training Loss: 0.149..  Training Accuracy: 0.972 Validation Loss: 0.094..  Validation Accuracy: 0.993
saving model...
Epoch: 15/20..  Training Loss: 0.110..  Training Accuracy: 0.976 Validation Loss: 0.091..  Validation Accuracy: 0.993
Epoch: 16/20..  Training Loss: 0.107..  Training Accuracy: 0.986 Validation Loss: 0.096..  Validation Accuracy: 0.993
Epoch: 17/20..  Training Loss: 0.132..  Training Accuracy: 0.978 Validation Loss: 0.100..  Validation Accuracy: 0.993
saving model...
Epoch: 18/20..  Training Loss: 0.126..  Training Accuracy: 0.980 Validation Loss: 0.089..  Validation Accuracy: 0.993
Epoch: 19/20..  Training Loss: 0.122..  Training Accuracy: 0.984 Validation Loss: 0.093..  Validation Accuracy: 0.993
Epoch: 20/20..  Training Loss: 0.112..  Training Accuracy: 0.975 Validation Loss: 0.096..  Validation Accuracy: 0.993
saving model...
Epoch: 20/20..  Training Loss: 0.077..  Training Accuracy: 0.987 Validation Loss: 0.081..  Validation Accuracy: 0.993
Finish!
```

FIGURE 6.23 "Training Accuracy" is 98.7% and "Validation Accuracy" is 99.3% after training the model for 20 epochs using a batch size of 64.

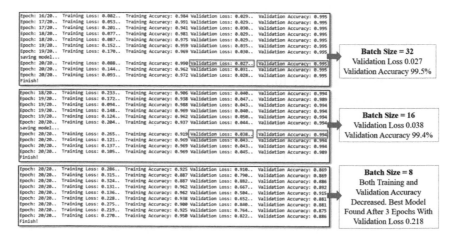

FIGURE 6.24 Training and validation accuracies and losses for different batch sizes (32, 16, and 8) when other parameters remain unchanged.

Figure 6.24 shows the training performance for batch sizes 32, 16, and 8. Here, we observe that decreasing the batch size improves model performance. However, for smaller batch sizes, the model becomes unstable, and performance starts to decline. Typically, an increase in batch size should be compensated with different learning rates [16]. So, depending on the GPU's capacity, users should fine-tune the model by changing batch size, learning rate, epochs, etc. For this case study, we can assume that if other variables are the same as the example code, a batch size of 32 exhibits better model performance.

6.9.2 Using a Different Optimizer

In this case study, PyTorch's Stochastic Gradient Descent (SGD) optimizer is used (Figure 6.15) to minimize the cost function of the network. SGD is the most common optimizer for linear regression or classification problems and is also suitable for small or medium-sized datasets. However, the "torch.optim" package has a variety of optimizers, such as Adadelta, Adagrad, Adam, RMSprop, etc. A list of all optimizers that are available in PyTorch can be checked from [12]. Each of these optimizers has its pros and cons, and the selection of a good optimizer typically depends on the complexity of tasks and the size of the dataset. An article published in [17] highlights essential tips for selecting the best optimizer. We may try out different optimizers in this case study to check changes in the accuracies and losses of the deep learning model. For example, the adaptive learning rate-based optimizer "Adagrad" can be used by importing it from PyTorch's optimization library [18]. In that scenario, only the code section that imports the SGD optimizer (optim.SGD) from Figure 6.15 can be commented out using a hashmark, and the optimizer importing the "Adagrad" library can be added. Figure 6.25 shows this updated code and the accuracy/losses for this new optimizer. Also, the Python code using this optimizer (main_AdagradOptimizer.py) is available in the additional resources folder.

The learning rate schedulers can also be altered for fine-tuning purposes. This case study uses a "StepLR" scheduler with step size 5 and gamma 0.3 for learning rate decay. However, other forms of schedulers, such as MultistepLR, ExponentialLR, PolynomialLR, CyclicLR, etc., can also be considered. It is recommended to check different schedulers and tweak their internal parameters, such as the step size (period of learning

```
model = nn.DataParallel(model) # use this for multiple GPU
model= model.cuda()

#define loss function, optimizer, and scheduler
criterion = nn.CrossEntropyLoss().cuda()
#optimizer = optim.SGD(model.parameters(),lr = config.lr,momentum=0.9,weight_decay=1e-4)
optimizer = optim.Adagrad(model.parameters(), lr=0.05)

scheduler = optim.lr_scheduler.StepLR(optimizer,step_size=5,gamma=0.3)

## you can manually freeze ot unfreeze the weights of a model. To freeze the model set
## param.requires_grad = False
for param in model.parameters():
    param.requires_grad = True
```

```
Epoch: 10/20.. Training Loss: 0.739.. Training Accuracy: 0.822 Validation Loss: 0.589.. Validation Accuracy: 0.819
saving model...
Epoch: 12/20.. Training Loss: 0.646.. Training Accuracy: 0.820 Validation Loss: 0.573.. Validation Accuracy: 0.819
saving model...
Epoch: 14/20.. Training Loss: 0.610.. Training Accuracy: 0.831 Validation Loss: 0.549.. Validation Accuracy: 0.823
Epoch: 15/20.. Training Loss: 0.654.. Training Accuracy: 0.807 Validation Loss: 0.553.. Validation Accuracy: 0.823
saving model...
Epoch: 17/20.. Training Loss: 0.657.. Training Accuracy: 0.822 Validation Loss: 0.543.. Validation Accuracy: 0.823
Epoch: 19/20.. Training Loss: 0.622.. Training Accuracy: 0.827 Validation Loss: 0.546.. Validation Accuracy: 0.823
Epoch: 20/20.. Training Loss: 0.657.. Training Accuracy: 0.821 Validation Loss: 0.548.. Validation Accuracy: 0.823
Finish!
```

FIGURE 6.25 Changing optimizer types from SGD to Adagrad would result in different accuracies and losses.

```
model = nn.DataParallel(model) # use this for multiple GPU
model= model.cuda()

#define loss function, optimizer, and scheduler
criterion = nn.CrossEntropyLoss().cuda()
optimizer = optim.SGD(model.parameters(),lr = config.lr,momentum=0.9,weight_decay=1e-4)
#optimizer = optim.Adagrad(model.parameters(), lr=0.05)

#scheduler = optim.lr_scheduler.StepLR(optimizer,step_size=5,gamma=0.3)
scheduler = optim.lr_scheduler.StepLR(optimizer,step_size=10,gamma=0.5)

## you can manually freeze ot unfreeze the weights of a model. To freeze the model set
## param.requires_grad = False
for param in model.parameters():
    param.requires_grad = True
```

Change the Step Size and gamma in scheduler

```
Epoch: 10/20..  Training Loss: 0.179..  Training Accuracy: 0.971 Validation Loss: 0.191..  Validation Accuracy: 0.975
saving model...
Epoch: 12/20..  Training Loss: 0.150..  Training Accuracy: 0.976 Validation Loss: 0.172..  Validation Accuracy: 0.979
saving model...
Epoch: 14/20..  Training Loss: 0.139..  Training Accuracy: 0.972 Validation Loss: 0.168..  Validation Accuracy: 0.979
saving model...
Epoch: 15/20..  Training Loss: 0.113..  Training Accuracy: 0.984 Validation Loss: 0.120..  Validation Accuracy: 0.979
saving model...
Epoch: 17/20..  Training Loss: 0.109..  Training Accuracy: 0.980 Validation Loss: 0.089..  Validation Accuracy: 0.990
Epoch: 19/20..  Training Loss: 0.079..  Training Accuracy: 0.991 Validation Loss: 0.090..  Validation Accuracy: 0.990
Epoch: 20/20..  Training Loss: 0.075..  Training Accuracy: 0.990 Validation Loss: 0.092..  Validation Accuracy: 0.990
Finish!
```

FIGURE 6.26 Change in training and validation accuracies when the step size and gamma parameters are changed in the "StepLR" scheduler.

rate decay) and the gamma (a multiplication factor for learning rate), to improve the model performance. A guide for using various types of learning rate schedulers is described in [19]. Figure 6.26 shows the change in model performance when the step size in the "StepLR" scheduler is increased to 10, and the gamma is increased to 0.5.

6.10 SIMILAR APPLICATIONS FOR ENGINEERS

This chapter presents a case study of the image classification problem using deep learning. The image dataset used here is freely available on Kaggel's site, and it is highly recommended that readers of this book try running the model using the same dataset. Once familiar with the program structures, readers should try importing and comparing various other pretrained models to classify the images. Also, careful considerations are needed while altering the hyperparameters for fine-tuning.

In the engineering fields, there are a lot of real-life image classification problems available where deep transfer learning can be implemented. A few examples are face or fingerprint recognition for security lock systems, types of cracks or failures (such as fatigue, tensile, or compressive) recognition in machines or structures, cancer or tumor cell detection from X-ray/ultrasound images, and much more. Readers can also make their own image datasets for computer vision-based research or design projects and implement deep learning for classifications.

The following section presents programming questions related to using different types of optimizers and hyperparameter tunings.

6.11 EXERCISE PROBLEM

1. In this chapter, the "Traffic Sign Detection" dataset from Kaggle's site is used for classifications [1]. The case study shows the implementations of "SGD" and "Adagrad" optimizers that achieve different model performances. Use PyTorch's "Adam" optimizer to do the same road sign classifications by keeping all other variables the same as the case study and determine the training/validation losses. Does the model show better performance?

2. Run problem 1 of this section for 256 batch size and 30 epochs and comment on the change in model performance.

3. Use the case study program with "SGD" optimizer but change the learning scheduler from "StepLR" to "PolynomialLR" that decays the learning rate using a polynomial function of power 1 (power = 1.0) in 10 iterations (total_ires=10). Does the "PolynomialLR" scheduler return better performance than "StepLR"?

4. Run problem 3 of this section using various powers of "PolynomialLR" schedulers. How an increasing power of the polynomial function affects the model performance?

5. Use "ResNet34" model instead of "ResNet50" in the program. Which one provides better model performance?

REFERENCES

1. LARXEL, 2020, "Road Sign Detection," https://www.kaggle.com/datasets/andrewmvd/road-sign-detection.
2. He, K., Zhang, X., Ren, S., and Sun, J., "Deep Residual Learning for Image Recognition," Proceedings of the IEEE Conference on Computer Vision and Pattern Recognition, pp. 770–778.
3. Soumith Chintala, G. C., Dzhulgakov, D., Yang, E., and Shulga, N., 2023, "PyTorch," https://github.com/pytorch/pytorch.
4. Pedregosa, F., Varoquaux, G., Gramfort, A., Michel, V., Thirion, B., Grisel, O., Blondel, M., Prettenhofer, P., Weiss, R., Dubourg, V., Vanderplas, J., Passos, A., Cournapeau, D., Brucher, M., Perrot, M., Duchesnay, E., and Louppe, G., 2012, "Scikit-Learn: Machine Learning in Python," Journal of Machine Learning Research, 12, pp. 2825–2830.

5. Bradski, G., 2000, "The OpenCV Library," https://opencv.org/.
6. PyTorch, 2023, "Transforming and augmenting images," https://pytorch.org/vision/stable/transforms.html.
7. imgaug, 2020, "Overview of augmenters."
8. 2023, "Transforming and augmenting images," https://pytorch.org/vision/stable/transforms.html#torchvision.transforms.ToTensor.
9. PyTorch, 2023, "ResNet50," https://pytorch.org/vision/main/models/generated/torchvision.models.resnet50.html#torchvision.models.resnet50.
10. 2023, "TORCH.UTILS.DATA," https://pytorch.org/docs/stable/data.html.
11. 2023, "PyTorch - TORCH.NN," https://pytorch.org/docs/stable/nn.html?highlight=torch+nn#module-torch.nn.
12. 2023, "PyTorch TORCH.OPTIM," https://pytorch.org/docs/stable/optim.html.
13. Bushaev, V., 2017, "Stochastic Gradient Descent with momentum," https://towardsdatascience.com/stochastic-gradient-descent-with-momentum-a84097641a5d.
14. Kumar, A., 2022, "Weight Decay in Machine Learning: Concepts," https://vitalflux.com/weight-decay-in-machine-learning-concepts/.
15. Prechelt, L., 2012, "Early Stopping—But When?," Neural Networks: Tricks of the Trade: 2nd Ed., G. Montavon, G. B. Orr, and K.-R. Müller, eds., Springer, Berlin, Heidelberg, pp. 53–67.
16. Devansh, 2022, "How does Batch Size impact your model learning," https://medium.com/geekculture/how-does-batch-size-impact-your-model-learning-2dd34d9fb1fa.
17. Giordano, D., 2020, "7 tips to choose the best optimizer," https://towardsdatascience.com/7-tips-to-choose-the-best-optimizer-47bb9c1219e.
18. Duchi, J., Hazan, E., and Singer, Y., 2011, "Adaptive Subgradient Methods for Online Learning and Stochastic Optimization," Journal of Machine Learning Research, 12, pp. 2121–2159.
19. Monigatti, L., 2022, "A Visual Guide to Learning Rate Schedulers in PyTorch," https://towardsdatascience.com/a-visual-guide-to-learning-rate-schedulers-in-pytorch-24bbb262c863.

## CHAPTER 7

Case Study II

Object Detection

7.1 PROBLEM STATEMENT

Case Study II demonstrates a practical implementation of deep learning for object detection problems. In this case study, we have used the Faster R-CNN (Region-based Convolutional Neural Network) model that uses a Region Proposal network (RPN) for greater efficiency and speeds during object detection [1]. The Faster R-CNN is an improvement from Fast R-CNN that differs from the original R-CNN and utilizes a single network to both classify objects and create bounding boxes using Region of Interest (RoI) pooling layers [2]. To train and test our model, an open-source dataset containing 1001 images for training and 175 images for testing is used. All of the images show one or multiple cars on the road or only roads without any cars. The dataset is available on Kaggle's site and can be downloaded from [3].

The "Car Object Detection" data provides rectangular bounding box dimensions in the train_solution_bounding_boxes.csv file for images that have cars in it. Some image has multiple cars in it, and in that case, the image name appears multiple times in the .csv file. If an image doesn't have any car in it, its name isn't included in the .csv file. The goal of Case Study II is to train a deep learning model using the given images with bounding boxes and evaluate the trained model. If trained properly, the model should be able to detect car(s) in an image and create dimension points (xmin, xmax, ymin, and ymax) for the bounding box(s). We recommend

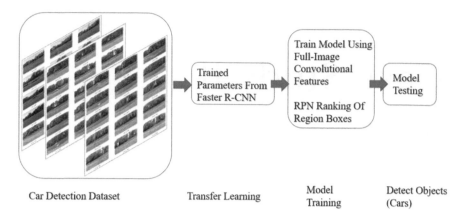

FIGURE 7.1 Schematic of transfer learning using Faster R-CNN for object detection.

readers of this book download the dataset from Kaggle and reproduce the results by following the instructions given in Chapter 5 (for GPU setup) and executing the codes given in this chapter.

A schematic of the transfer learning process using the pre-trained network (Faster R-CNN) is shown in Figure 7.1. After successful training and testing on the data set, we have used several random pictures of cars on the road (downloaded from online) to evaluate the performance of the deep learning model on unseen images.

In the following sections, Python codes for the training and testing operations are explained. All of the codes presented in this chapter are written and tested using Spyder Integrated Developed Environment (IDE) from Anaconda. Note that the Spyder IDE should be opened using Anaconda Navigator or by executing the "spyder" command in "Anaconda Prompt". Otherwise, the program may not find the required CUDA environment for PyTorch, and the "torch.cuda.is_available()" command in Spyder's console will return "False".

7.2 DEFINING DEFAULT CONFIGURATION

The first task is to create Python classes that can group similar types of data and functions. The "Class" in Python forms an object to maintain a set of attributes. Here, in this program, a new class variable (DefaultConfigs) is created to set or define important default parameters (objects) that can be used throughout the program. The "DefaultConfigs" class is called using a variable named "config" (Figure 7.2), and all of the class attributes can be accessed using the reference operator dot, ".". Here, declared class objects

```
class DefaultConfigs(object):
    Image_PATH = r"C:\Users\tariqarif\Desktop\Car Detection\archive\data\training_images"
    Test_PATH = r"C:\Users\tariqarif\Desktop\Car Detection\archive\data\testing_images"
    Annot_PATH = r"C:\Users\tariqarif\Desktop\Car Detection\archive\data"
    Model_PATH = r"C:\Users\tariqarif\Desktop\Car Detection\archive"
    num_classes = 1
    img_width = 256
    img_height = 256
    channels = 3
    lr = 0.001
    batch_size = 16
    epochs = 10
    seed= 43

config = DefaultConfigs()
```

FIGURE 7.2   Create a "DefaultConfigs" class to define parameters that will be used throughout the program.

"Image_PATH", "Test_PATH", "Annot_PATH", and "Model_PATH" are to assign data locations for training images, testing images, annotations files, and saving the best model, respectively. The "num_classes", "img_width", "img_height", "channels", "lr" (learning rate), "batch_size", "epochs", and, "seed" are defined to assign default numerical values.

7.3 RANDOM SEED AND IMPORT MODULES/LIBRARIES

In this section, major modules and libraries required for running deep learning are presented. First, we import Python's "random", "numpy", and "torch" libraries. Then a function "set_all_random_seed" is defined to set random seeds of "numpy" and "torch" using the default seed assigned in Figure 7.2. Figure 7.3 shows the commands in Spyder editor for importing these libraries and creating the function.

To read the data from the dataset and to create a data frame "pandas" library is imported. Figure 7.4 shows the Python code for creating a data

```
#import libraries to set random seeds
import random
import numpy as np
import torch

def set_all_random_seed(seed = config.seed):
    random.seed(seed)
    np.random.seed(seed)
    torch.manual_seed(seed)
    torch.cuda.manual_seed_all(seed)
    return seed

print(f'random seed {set_all_random_seed()}')
```

FIGURE 7.3   Import the "random", "numpy", and "torch" libraries and define the "set_all_random_seed" function.

```
############################
#import Librarie to read in data and create dataframe
import pandas as pd          #to create dataframe object

df = pd.read_csv(config.Annot_PATH+'/train_solution_bounding_boxes.csv')
image_names = [i for i in df['image'].unique()]
#########################################################
#split the dataset into train and validation sets
from sklearn.model_selection import train_test_split
train_data_list,valid_data_list = train_test_split(image_names,test_size = 0.20,random_state = config.seed)
#############################
#prepare the dataset
from torch.utils.data import Dataset
from torchvision import transforms as T    # to transform the data into a tensor and normalize it
import cv2                                  # to read image files and process
from imgaug import augmenters as iaa        # to perform image augmentation
from imgaug.augmentables.bbs import BoundingBox, BoundingBoxesOnImage
```

FIGURE 7.4 Import "pandas", "train_test_split", "Dataset", "transforms", "cv2", "augmenters", and "BoundingBox" and create a data frame.

frame using image names. The "unique()" method is used to read only the unique names of images.

After storing the data in "image_names", the "sklearn.model_selection" class is used to pre-process data for training. All data were randomly divided into training and testing datasets using the "train_test_split()" method. Figure 7.4 shows this data split where the test data size is 20% of the total data. An integer (config.seed) 43 is assigned to "random_state" so that the code can reproduce identical outputs later. The "Dataset" library is for maintaining the data set effectively during the training process [4], "transform" for transforming images [5], open cv for reading image files, "augmenters" for implementing image augmentation sequences such as crop, horizontal/vertical flips, pooling, and gaussian blurs [6], "BoundingBox" library is for importing car locations in training images. The commands for importing these libraries and modules are shown in Figure 7.4.

7.4 DEFINE DATASET CLASS AND ATTRIBUTES

A new class variable called "CarDataset" is defined that has six different attributes. These are "images_df", "images_names", "mean", "std", "augment", and "mode". These attribute assignments are shown in Figure 7.5. The "__init__" method is used for setting up the initial value of the instance, and the "__len__" method returns the number of image items in the "images_names", and the "__getitem__" method read images using indices and bounding boxes for training. The "augmentor()" method is utilized by "__getitem__" to aid the artificial image generations. It also uses "ToTensor()" to convert the "ndarray" (image features) to tensors and scale pixel intensity values from 0 to 1 [7]. A "target" dictionary is created to store data values for "boxes", "labels", "area", and "iscrowed" as shown in Figure 7.5.

```
class CarDataset(Dataset):
    def __init__(self,images_df,image_names,mean,std,augment=True,mode="train"):
        self.images_df = images_df.copy()
        self.image_names = image_names.copy()
        self.mean = mean
        self.std = std
        self.augment = augment
        self.mode = mode
    def __len__(self):
        return len(self.image_names)

    def __getitem__(self,index):
        X,boxes = self.read_images(index)
        if self.augment:
            X,boxes = self.augmentor(X,boxes)

        X = T.Compose([T.ToTensor(),T.Normalize(self.mean, self.std)])(X.copy())
        boxes = torch.as_tensor(boxes, dtype=torch.float32)
        y = torch.ones((len(boxes),), dtype=torch.int64)
        area = (boxes[:, 3] - boxes[:, 1]) * (boxes[:, 2] - boxes[:, 0])
        iscrowd = torch.zeros((len(boxes),), dtype=torch.int64)
        image_id = torch.tensor([index])

        target = {}
        target["boxes"] = boxes
        target["labels"] = y
        target["image_id"] = image_id
        target["area"] = area
        target["iscrowd"] = iscrowd
        return X.float(), target
```

FIGURE 7.5 The "CarDataset" class and "__init__", "__len__", "__getitem__" methods.

A method called "read_images" is created to read, normalize, and rescale images. It reads images from the path defined by "config.Image_ PATH" and converts the color channel from BGR to RGB. These images are resized into default image weight/height as defined by default configurations and transformed along with bound boxes given for every image (Figure 7.6).

In order to increase the number of training images, an image augmentation technique is applied. The image augmentation generally improves the model performance as it increases the original number of images available in the dataset. We have used the "augmentor" method to rotate images 90, 180, and 270 degrees, shear images by −16 to 16 degrees, and apply flip operations to 50% of images. These operations are done in random order (one of the operations is selected each time randomly) by setting the "random_order" to "True" as shown in Figure 7.7. One difference in this "augmentor" method compared to that of classification case study is that it incorporates an array (bbs_array) to store box dimensions after augmentation.

```python
def read_images(self,index):
    img_id = self.image_names[index]
    filename = str(config.Image_PATH+ '/' +img_id)
    image = cv2.imread(filename)
    height,width,_ = image.shape
    image = cv2.cvtColor(image, cv2.COLOR_BGR2RGB)
    image = image/255.0  #normalize the image
    image = cv2.resize(image,(config.img_width,config.img_height))

    row = self.images_df.loc[self.images_df.image==img_id].copy()
    xmin = row.xmin.values
    ymin = row.ymin.values
    xmax = row.xmax.values
    ymax = row.ymax.values

    x_scale = config.img_width/width
    y_scale = config.img_height/height

    xmin = xmin*x_scale
    ymin = ymin*y_scale
    xmax = xmax*x_scale
    ymax = ymax*y_scale

    boxes = []
    for i in range(len(xmin)):
        #getting boxes as a list of lists
        boxes.append([xmin[i],ymin[i],xmax[i],ymax[i]])

    return image, boxes
```

FIGURE 7.6 "read_image" method to read and pre-process images and bounding boxes.

```python
def augmentor(self,image,boxes):
    bboxes = [BoundingBox(x1=box[0], y1= box[1], x2=box[2], y2=box[3]) for box in boxes]
    bbs = BoundingBoxesOnImage(bboxes,shape=image.shape)
    seq = iaa.Sequential([
        iaa.OneOf([
            iaa.Affine(rotate=90),
            iaa.Affine(rotate=180),
            iaa.Affine(rotate=270),
            iaa.Affine(shear=(-16, 16)),
            iaa.Fliplr(0.5),
        ])], random_order=True)

    image_aug, bbs_aug = seq(image=image, bounding_boxes=bbs)
    bbs_array = bbs_aug.to_xyxy_array()

    boxes = []
    for box in bbs_array:
        boxes.append([box[0],box[1],box[2],box[3]])

    return image_aug, boxes
```

FIGURE 7.7 "augmentor" function for applying one of the operations randomly: rotate an image 90, 180, and 270 degrees, shear by -16 to 16 degrees, or apply flip operations. The "augmentor" function also stores updated transformed bounding boxes for images.

7.5 LOAD DATASET AND MODEL ARCHITECTURE

The "mean" and "std" variables are defined that are specific to the Faster R-CNN model. To process the data batches faster and receive a list of tuples, the "collate_fn" function is created. The data loading utility of PyTorch, the "DataLoader" constructor is used with arguments for dataset ("train_gen"), batch size, shuffling, pin memory, and collate function. This constructor wraps an iterable around the defined dataset ("train_gen" or "val_gen") and facilitates easy access to the images. Detailed explanations of these arguments are explained in [8]. The validation testing is also done using the "DataLoader" but on the validation dataset without shuffling (Figure 7.8).

After the data set is imported and pre-processed, the next step would be training and testing the deep learning network. At this stage, we need to import the packages required for the Faster R-CNN model. The "optim" and "torchvision" modules of PyTorch are imported. The "optim" module can be used to implement different optimization algorithms and the "torchvision" module have popular datasets and model architectures [9]. The pre-trained model "fastercnn_resnet50_fpn" is imported from "torchvision.models" with default weights, and the "FastRCNNPredictor" class is imported to change the number of output classes according to requirements. The model is also transformed for data manipulation, making it suitable for training. After loading the model, if we check it in the Spyder's console window (by entering "model"), it will return its internal architecture. There in the last linear layer, the model expects 1024 input features and 91 output features (in_features = 1024). These feature numbers need to be changed for transfer learning. The model is updated using "modcl.roi_hcads.box_prcdictor" for the expected output of our case study, where the total number of output classes is two (1 for car and 1 for background).

```
# check the model, and use the appropriate mean and std values that the model expects
mean=[0.485, 0.456, 0.406]
std=[0.229, 0.224, 0.225]

############################
#create dataloader object to iterate over the datasets
from torch.utils.data import DataLoader

def collate_fn(batch):
    return tuple(zip(*batch))

train_gen = CarDataset(df,train_data_list,mean,std,augment=True,mode="train")
train_loader = DataLoader(train_gen,batch_size=config.batch_size,shuffle=True,pin_memory=True,num_workers=0,collate_fn=collate_fn)
val_gen = CarDataset(df,valid_data_list,mean,std,augment=False,mode="eval")
val_loader = DataLoader(val_gen,batch_size=config.batch_size,shuffle=False,pin_memory=True,collate_fn=collate_fn)
```

FIGURE 7.8   Define model parameters, collate function, and "DataLoader" constructor to facilitate easy access to training and validation datasets.

```
# model
from torch import optim
import torchvision
from torchvision.models.detection.faster_rcnn import FastRCNNPredictor

model = torchvision.models.detection.fasterrcnn_resnet50_fpn(weights="DEFAULT")
model.transform

in_features = model.roi_heads.box_predictor.cls_score.in_features
model.roi_heads.box_predictor = FastRCNNPredictor(in_features, (config.num_classes+1)) # +1 for background
model= model.cuda()

optimizer = optim.SGD(model.parameters(),lr=config.lr,momentum=0.9, weight_decay=0.0005)
scheduler = torch.optim.lr_scheduler.StepLR(optimizer,step_size=5,gamma=0.5) #after 5 epochs, the learning rate will be halved

#may run first 10 epochs without setting the gradients to True, then run more epochs with True setting
for param in model.parameters():
    param.requires_grad = True        .
```

FIGURE 7.9   Setting up imported model for transfer learning and defining optimizer and scheduler.

Next, the Stochastic Gradient Descent (SGD) optimizer is defined using model parameters, learning rate, momentum, and weight decay. The momentum and weight decay are optional parameters that minimize the impact of noises in convergence and improve the generalization performance of the model [10, 11]. The "StepLR" scheduler is used with ten step size with a multiplicative factor of 0.5 to reduce the learning rate by half after five epochs. Finally, the "requires_grad" is set to True for instructing automatic differentiation or "autograd" recording operation (Figure 7.9).

It is recommended to launch Spyder IDE from "Anacoda Prompt" by entering the command "spyder" and running each of the program sections separately or line by line. For example, to run a section of the program in Spyder IDE (Windows), we may select multiple lines of code and press the "F9" button. This process will help the user to understand the codes step-by-step and pinpoint an error quickly. This case study example uses a single GPU (GeForce RTX 3090), and data parallelism to split the batches is not utilized.

7.6 MODEL TRAINING AND SAVING THE BEST MODEL

Now the model is ready for training. A nested "for loop" is used to run the model for a number of epochs set by the default configurations ("config. epochs"). In this case study, the model is going to run for ten epochs. Figure 7.10 shows the code for training the model on a single CUDA using forward and back propagation and calculating loss in every iteration. A "step_check" variable is created to save the best model in every two iterations. Initially, the best loss is set to a very large number (np.inf), and after every iteration, the program updates this best loss if a lower loss value is found. For this object detection problem, total training loss is the summation of bounding box loss, object detection loss, regional proposal network

```python
#training
steps = 0 #track the iterations
step_check = 2 #check losses and save best model (if loss decreases) after 2 iterations
best_loss= np.inf
for epoch in range(config.epochs):
    model.train();
    train_losses = 0
    box_losses = 0
    class_losses = 0
    object_losses = 0
    rpn_losses = 0
    for images, targets in iter(train_loader):
        images = list(image.cuda() for image in images)
        targets = [{k: torch.tensor(v).cuda() for k, v in t.items()} for t in targets]
        loss_dict = model(images, targets)
        #del loss_dict['loss_classifier'] # if wants to remove clssification loss
        losses = sum(loss for loss in loss_dict.values())
        optimizer.zero_grad()
        losses.backward()
        optimizer.step()
        steps += 1
        train_losses += sum(loss for loss in loss_dict.values()).detach()
        box_losses += loss_dict['loss_box_reg'].detach()
        object_losses += loss_dict['loss_objectness'].detach()
        rpn_losses += loss_dict['loss_rpn_box_reg'].detach()
        class_losses += loss_dict['loss_classifier'].detach()

        if steps % step_check == 0:
            if train_losses < best_loss:
                best_loss = train_losses
                print('saving model...')
                torch.save(model, config.Model_PATH+'/model.pt')
            print("Epoch: {}/{}.. ".format(epoch+1, config.epochs),
                  "Box Regression Loss: {:.3f}.. ".format(box_losses),
                  "Objectness Loss: {:.3f}.. ".format(object_losses),
                  "RPN Box Regression loss: {:.3f}.. ".format(rpn_losses),
                  "Classification Loss: {:.3f}.. ".format(class_losses),
                  "Training Loss: {:.3f}.. ".format(train_losses),
                  )
            train_losses = 0
            box_losses = 0
            class_losses = 0
            object_losses = 0
            rpn_losses = 0
    scheduler.step()
print('Finish!')
```

FIGURE 7.10   Model training and saving the best in every two iterations.

(RPN) loss, and classification loss. The code for this training process and printing the epoch numbers, training loss/accuracy, and validation loss/accuracy are shown in Figure 7.10.

The model training may return the "OutOfMemoryError: CUDA out of memory" error, which is an issue of GPU memory limitations. In that situation, the code won't execute, but the user can resolve this problem by reducing the batch size or image size (img_width and img_height). Sometimes, restarting the kernel in the Spyder console may solve the out-of-memory issue.

```
Epoch: 9/10..  Box Regression Loss: 0.215..  Objectness Loss: 0.010..  RPN Box Regression Loss: 0.006..  Classification Loss: 0.092..  Training Loss: 0.323..
Epoch: 9/10..  Box Regression Loss: 0.263..  Objectness Loss: 0.003..  RPN Box Regression Loss: 0.006..  Classification Loss: 0.104..  Training Loss: 0.376..
Epoch: 9/10..  Box Regression Loss: 0.216..  Objectness Loss: 0.005..  RPN Box Regression Loss: 0.004..  Classification Loss: 0.101..  Training Loss: 0.326..
Epoch: 10/10..  Box Regression Loss: 0.288..  Objectness Loss: 0.007..  RPN Box Regression Loss: 0.006..  Classification Loss: 0.113..  Training Loss: 0.413..
saving model...
Epoch: 10/10..  Box Regression Loss: 0.204..  Objectness Loss: 0.003..  RPN Box Regression Loss: 0.004..  Classification Loss: 0.087..  Training Loss: 0.298..
Epoch: 10/10..  Box Regression Loss: 0.257..  Objectness Loss: 0.008..  RPN Box Regression Loss: 0.006..  Classification Loss: 0.098..  Training Loss: 0.369..
Epoch: 10/10..  Box Regression Loss: 0.248..  Objectness Loss: 0.004..  RPN Box Regression Loss: 0.007..  Classification Loss: 0.105..  Training Loss: 0.364..
Epoch: 10/10..  Box Regression Loss: 0.270..  Objectness Loss: 0.009..  RPN Box Regression Loss: 0.006..  Classification Loss: 0.105..  Training Loss: 0.390..
Epoch: 10/10..  Box Regression Loss: 0.230..  Objectness Loss: 0.003..  RPN Box Regression Loss: 0.006..  Classification Loss: 0.092..  Training Loss: 0.330..
Epoch: 10/10..  Box Regression Loss: 0.217..  Objectness Loss: 0.004..  RPN Box Regression Loss: 0.004..  Classification Loss: 0.085..  Training Loss: 0.310..
Epoch: 10/10..  Box Regression Loss: 0.220..  Objectness Loss: 0.003..  RPN Box Regression Loss: 0.005..  Classification Loss: 0.090..  Training Loss: 0.318..
Epoch: 10/10..  Box Regression Loss: 0.256..  Objectness Loss: 0.007..  RPN Box Regression Loss: 0.007..  Classification Loss: 0.116..  Training Loss: 0.386..
Finish!
```

FIGURE 7.11 The best training loss is 0.98, and the classification loss is 0.087 after training the model for 10 epochs.

Once the model runs and starts to train, we will get the box regression, objectness, RPN, and classification losses. The model determines the training losses as the summation of all four losses and saves the parameters that provide minimum training loss. In this case study, the training and validation datasets are randomly split, where the allocated training and validation images are 80% and 20% of the total images, respectively. After 10 epochs, we find a minimum training loss of 0.98 (Figure 7.11). During training, if we find the best training loss within the first one or two epochs and after that loss increases randomly, the training should be terminated as it indicates that the model is failing to generalize the dataset and is overfitting.

7.7 MODEL TESTING AND INFERENCE

We may test the model performance by detecting car images from the dataset manually. Figures 7.12 and 7.13 show the code required to load the trained model from "config.Model_PATH", check an image from the "val_loader" batch, and predict the bounding boxes using the trained model. For plotting the bounding box over the image, "imshow" command from "matplotlib.pyplot" is used. The "imshow" plots all the bounding boxes that have prediction scores over 90%. Figure 7.12 shows the prediction over the "val_loader" image number 2 and 5.

The testing shown in this section indicates that the model can learn from the dataset and detect cars reasonably well. Results for a few other index images from the validation dataset are shown in Figure 7.13.

Now we do the model inference using entirely new images in the real-world context. To test this, four different open-source pictures are downloaded from https://unsplash.com/. These pictures are renamed (e.g., Test1. jpg, Test2.jpg, Test3.jpg, and Test4.jpg) and available in the additional resources of this chapter. In our workstation, the images are saved into

For im_no = 2

```
#Load the saved model
model = torch.load(config.Model_PATH+'/model.pt')
model.eval();
##########################
# Display image and label.
import matplotlib.pyplot as plt
from torchvision.utils import draw_bounding_boxes
features, labels = next(iter(val_loader))
#print(f"Feature batch shape: {features.size()}")
#print(f"Labels batch shape: {labels.size()}")
im_no = 2
image = [features[im_no].cuda()]
output = model(image)
prediction = output[0]

img = features[im_no].permute(1,2,0).numpy()
img = (mean + img *std)
img_show = torch.tensor(img* 255, dtype=torch.uint8).permute(2,0,1)
img = features[im_no]

iou_thresh= 0.2
keep = torchvision.ops.nms(prediction['boxes'], prediction['scores'], iou_thresh)

prediction['boxes'] = prediction['boxes'][keep]
prediction['scores'] = prediction['scores'][keep]
prediction['labels'] = prediction['labels'][keep]

plt.imshow(draw_bounding_boxes(img_show,
    prediction['boxes'][prediction['scores'] > 0.9], width=4).permute(1, 2, 0))
```

Output →

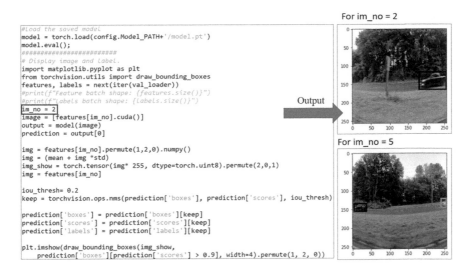

For im_no = 5

FIGURE 7.12   Creating bounding boxes for cars from the validation image dataset using the trained model and displaying the image with bounding boxes for index images 2 and 5.

the Desktop's "Car Detection" Folder, as shown in Figure 7.14. First, the inference images are normalized and processed for prediction. The image "imshow" command from "matplotlib.pyplot" is used with prediction scores over 50% for plotting the bounding boxes on the images. The prediction scores should be fine-tuned and optimized for variations of data. Typically, the trained model can predict with a higher confidence level if the image features and outlooks are similar to the dataset images. For outside images, this score should be lowered (e.g., 0.5, 0.3, etc.) to detect objects correctly, as shown in Figure 7.14.

For im_no = 6   For im_no = 12   For im_no = 15

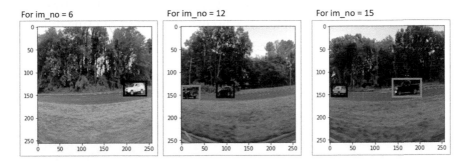

FIGURE 7.13   Displaying images with bounding boxes for index images 6, 12, and 15 using the trained model.

```
path = r"C:\Users\tariqarif\Desktop\Car Detection"

image = cv2.imread(path+"Test1.jpg")
image = cv2.cvtColor(image, cv2.COLOR_BGR2RGB)
image = image/255.0
image = cv2.resize(image,(config.img_width,config.img_height))
X = T.Compose([T.ToTensor(),T.Normalize(mean, std)])(image.copy())
X = X.float().cuda()
output = model([X])
prediction = output[0]

img = X.cpu().permute(1,2,0).numpy()
img = (mean + img *std)
img_show = torch.tensor(img* 255, dtype=torch.uint8).permute(2,0,1)

iou_thresh= 0.2
keep = torchvision.ops.nms(prediction['boxes'], prediction['scores'], iou_thresh)

prediction['boxes'] = prediction['boxes'][keep]
prediction['scores'] = prediction['scores'][keep]
prediction['labels'] = prediction['labels'][keep]

plt.imshow(draw_bounding_boxes(img_show,
    prediction['boxes'][prediction['scores'] > 0.5], width=4).permute(1, 2, 0))
```

FIGURE 7.14   Model inference using test images downloaded from online.

Figure 7.15 demonstrates the car detections on test images. In "Test3. jpg" the model can't predict some small car images shown at the back. For this one, accuracy can be improved by reducing scores (e.g., 0.3).

7.7.1 Fine Tuning

For finding the optimal set of parameters, we recommended tweaking different parameters and evaluating the outputs that minimize the loss and improve training/inference time. We may update the codes of this chapter by changing batch size, epochs, learning rate, optimizer, schedulers, etc. To understand the effect of different hyperparameters on the model tuning, please refer to Sections 6.9.1 and 6.9.2 from Chapter 6. The exercise section of this chapter also discusses the effect of using different

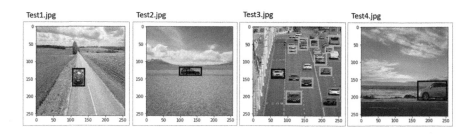

FIGURE 7.15   Trained model detecting cars from outside images for inference.

hyperparameters. We may also fine-tune the learning by using different pre-trained models. PyTorch has a variety of deep learning models that are pre-trained by others and available for public use [12]. Most of the models are trained on very large datasets that are labeled meticulously. Therefore, using those pre-trained models is beneficial as the model already has acquired knowledge and is able to apply that knowledge to specific tasks without making a fresh start. We may also customize the model parameters, such as nodes and layers inside the network, for fine-tuning the performance. Determining an optimum combination of hyperparameters for object detection is a matter of trial and error and should be evaluated with intuition by considering data types and computational power.

7.8 SIMILAR APPLICATIONS FOR ENGINEERS

This chapter presents a case study of object detection problems using deep learning. The image dataset used here is freely available on Kaggel's site, and it is highly recommended that readers of this book try running the model using the same dataset. In the engineering fields, many similar applications of object detection are found. Object detection is crucial for autonomous driving or flight so the system can perceive surrounding environments and make informed decisions. In robot manipulation tasks, using this technology, robots can grasp objects and move around in a dynamic environment. Other examples of practical object detection include tracking suspicious activities during surveillance, monitoring or counting products during manufacturing, detecting tumors and abnormal anatomy from medical imaging, monitoring wildlife or species in ecological analysis, etc.

The following section presents programming questions related to using different types of optimizers and hyperparameter tunings for object detection.

7.9 EXERCISE PROBLEM

1. In this chapter, the "Car Object Detection" dataset from Kaggle's site is used for detecting cars in an image, and this dataset can be downloaded from ref. [3]. The case study shows the implementation of using the Faster R-CNN model and finds an optimum training loss of 0.298 (Figure 7.11). Use a batch size of 8 images instead of 16 and comment on the loss and model performance using the new batch size.

2. In this case study, the learning scheduler "StepLR" is used with a Stochastic Gradient Descent (SGD) optimizer. The step size for

the scheduler is 5 with a multiplicative factor of 0.5 (step_size=5, gamma=0.5). i.e., the algorithm will reduce the learning rate by half after five epochs. How would the model training be affected if we reduce the learning rate by 80% (i.e., gamma = 0.2)?

3. The case study program uses the "fasterrcnn_resnet50_fpn" model with default weight for transfer learning. The PyTorch has other variations of this model that can also be used for object detection. Use the "Car Object Detection" dataset and train the "fasterrcnn_mobilenet_v3_large_fpn" model from PyTorch for object detection and compare its performance with the Faster R-CNN model.

4. Use the "Car Object Detection" dataset and train the "retinanet_resnet50_fpn" model from PyTorch with default weights for object detection and compare its performance with the Faster R-CNN model.

REFERENCES

1. Ren, S., He, K., Girshick, R., and Sun, J., 2017, "Faster R-CNN: Towards Real-Time Object Detection with Region Proposal Networks," IEEE Transactions on Pattern Analysis & Machine Intelligence, 39(06), pp. 1137–1149.
2. Girshick, R., 2015, "Fast R-CNN," Proceedings of the 2015 IEEE International Conference on Computer Vision (ICCV), IEEE Computer Society, pp. 1440–1448.
3. Zhang, E., 2022, "Car object detection," https://www.kaggle.com/datasets/sshikamaru/car-object-detection.
4. Soumith Chintala, G. C., Dzhulgakov, D., Yang, E., and Shulga, N., 2023, "PyTorch," https://github.com/pytorch/pytorch.
5. PyTorch, 2023, "Transforming and augmenting images," https://pytorch.org/vision/stable/transforms.html.
6. imgaug, 2020, "Overview of augmenters."
7. 2023, "Transforming and augmenting images," https://pytorch.org/vision/stable/transforms.html#torchvision.transforms.ToTensor.
8. 2023, "Torch.utils.data," https://pytorch.org/docs/stable/data.html.
9. 2023, "PyTorch torch.optim," https://pytorch.org/docs/stable/optim.html.
10. Bushaev, V., 2017, "Stochastic gradient descent with momentum," https://towardsdatascience.com/stochastic-gradient-descent-with-momentum-a84097641a5d.
11. Kumar, A., 2022, "Weight decay in machine learning: Concepts," https://vitalflux.com/weight-decay-in-machine-learning-concepts/.
12. PyTorch, 2023, "Models and pre-trained weights," https://pytorch.org/vision/stable/models.html.

## CHAPTER 8

Case Study III

Semantic Segmentation

8.1 PROBLEM STATEMENT

Case Study III demonstrates a practical implementation of deep learning for image segmentation problems. In this case study, we have used the DeepLabV3 model with ResNet50 backbone, which uses image-level features to the Atrous Spatial Pyramid Pooling (ASPP) module for effective image segmentation [1]. DeepLabV3 is a very popular model for image segmentation that can be combined with convolutional bases such as ResNets (Residual Networks) for better segmentation tasks and is available in PyTorch.

To train and test our model, an open-source dataset containing 400 semantic images from drones is used. The dataset provides labeled binary, classes, and colormap information. The creator of this dataset made it available on Kaggle's site and can be downloaded from [2]. The goal of this case study is to train a deep learning model using the semantic images with labeled data and evaluate the trained model. If trained properly, the model should be able to segment an aerial image into different classes. We recommend readers of this book download the dataset and reproduce the results by following the instructions given in Chapter 5 (for GPU setup) and executing the codes given in this chapter.

A schematic of the transfer learning process using the pre-trained network (DeepLabV3_ResNet50) is shown in Figure 8.1. After successful training and testing on the data set, we have used several random pictures

DOI: 10.1201/9781003402923-8

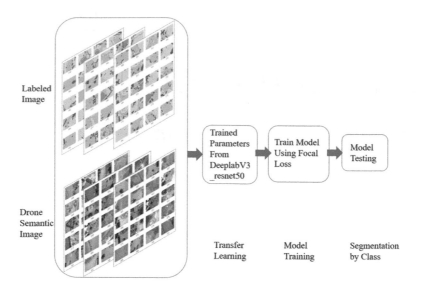

FIGURE 8.1   Schematic of transfer learning using DeepLabV3_ResNet50 for image segmentation.

of aerial images (downloaded from online) to evaluate the performance of the deep learning model on unseen images.

In the following sections, Python codes for the training and testing operations are explained. All of the codes presented in this chapter are written and executed using Spyder Integrated Developed Environment (IDE) from Anaconda. It is important to note that Spyder IDE should be opened using Anaconda Navigator or by executing the "spyder" command in "Anaconda Prompt". Otherwise, the program may not find the required CUDA environment for PyTorch, and the "torch.cuda.is_available()" command in Spyder's console will return "False".

8.2 DEFINING DEFAULT CONFIGURATION

The first task is to create Python classes that can group similar types of data and functions. The "Class" in Python forms an object to maintain a set of attributes. Here, in this program, a new class variable (DefaultConfigs) is created to set or define important default parameters (objects) that can be used throughout the program. The "DefaultConfigs" class is called using a variable named "config" (Figure 8.2), and all of the class attributes can be accessed using the reference operator dot, ".". Here, declared class objects "data_dir", "Image_PATH", and "Mask_PATH" are defined to assign data locations of "Segmentation", training images, and labeled images.

```
class DefaultConfigs(object):
    data_dir = r"C:\Users\tariqarif\Desktop\Segmentation"
    Image_PATH = '/archive/dataset/semantic_drone_dataset/original_images/'
    Mask_PATH = '/archive/dataset/semantic_drone_dataset/label_images_semantic/'
    num_classes = 23
    img_width = 512
    img_height = 512
    channels = 3
    lr = 0.001
    batch_size = 28
    epochs = 15
    seed= 43

config = DefaultConfigs()
```

FIGURE 8.2   Create a "DefaultConfigs" class to define parameters that will be used throughout the program.

The "num_classes", "img_width", "img_height", "channels", "lr" (learning rate), "batch_size", "epochs", and, "seed" are defined to assign default numerical values.

8.3 RANDOM SEED AND IMPORT MODULES/LIBRARIES

In this section, major modules and libraries required for running deep learning are presented. First, we import Python's "random", "numpy", and "torch" libraries. Then a function "set_all_random_seed" is defined to set random seeds of "numpy" and "torch" using the default seed assigned in Figure 8.2. Figure 8.3 shows the commands in Spyder editor for importing these libraries and the function.

To use operating system-dependent functionality Python's "os" module is imported. Also, to read the data from the dataset and to create a data frame, the "pandas" library is imported. Figure 8.4 shows the Python code for creating a data frame using an image list.

```
import random
import numpy as np
import torch

def set_all_random_seed(seed = config.seed): # to make the result reproducible
    random.seed(seed)
    np.random.seed(seed)
    torch.manual_seed(seed)
    torch.cuda.manual_seed_all(seed)
    return seed

print(f'random seed {set_all_random_seed()}')
```

FIGURE 8.3   Import the "random", "numpy", and "torch" libraries and define "set_all_random_seed" function.

```
import os
import pandas as pd

image_list = os.listdir(f'{config.data_dir}/{config.Image_PATH}')
image_list = [i[:-4] for i in image_list]
image_list = pd.DataFrame(image_list)
image_list.columns = ['filename']

#####################
from sklearn.model_selection import train_test_split
train_data_list,valid_data_list = train_test_split(image_list,test_size = 0.2,random_state = config.seed+1)
#####################
## Preprocess Dataset
import cv2
from torch.utils.data import Dataset
from torchvision import transforms as T
from imgaug import augmenters as iaa
from imgaug.augmentables.segmaps import SegmentationMapsOnImage
```

FIGURE 8.4   Import "os", "pandas", "train_test_split", "cv2", "Dataset", "transforms", "augmenters", and "SementationMapsOnImage" and create a data frame.

After creating the "image_list" data frame, the "sklearn.model_selection" class is used to pre-process data for training. All data were randomly divided into training and testing datasets using the "train_test_split()" method. Figure 8.4 shows the training images are split where the test data size is 20% of the total training data. An integer (config.seed+1) 44 is assigned to "random_state" so that the code can reproduce similar outputs later. The "Dataset" library for maintaining the data set effectively during the training process [3], "transform" for transforming images [4], "cv2" for reading image files [5], "augmenters" for implementing image augmentation sequences such as crop, horizontal/vertical flips, pooling [6], and "SegmentationMapsOnImage" for representing segmentation map for the corresponding image is imported [7]. The commands for importing these libraries and modules are shown in Figure 8.4.

8.4 DEFINE DATASET CLASS AND ATTRIBUTES

A new class variable called "DroneSegmentationDataset" is defined that has five different attributes. These are "images_df", "augment", "mode", "mean", and "std". These attribute assignments are shown in Figure 8.5. The "__init__" method is used for setting up the initial value of the instance, and the "__len__" method returns the number of image items in the image data frame, and the "__getitem__" method reads images and corresponding indices. The "augmentor()" method is utilized by "__getitem__" to aid the artificial image generations. "__getitem__" also uses "ToTensor()" to convert the "ndarray" (image features) to tensors and scale pixel intensity values from 0 to 1 [8]. The mask data are processed using the one-hot encoding that converts categorical data into a readable form for deep learning model architecture. During the pixel-wise segmentation task, a mask image might have different labels for representing different classes.

```
class DroneSegmentationDataset(Dataset):
    def __init__(self,images_df,mean,std,augment=True,mode="train"):
        self.image_df = images_df.copy()
        self.augment = augment
        self.mode = mode
        self.mean = mean
        self.std = std

    def __len__(self):
        return len(self.image_df)

    def __getitem__(self,index):
        X = self.read_images(index)
        mask = self.read_masks(index)

        if self.augment:
            X,mask = self.augmentor(X,mask)

        X = T.Compose([T.ToTensor(), T.Normalize(self.mean, self.std)])(X.copy())

        mask =  torch.from_numpy(mask.astype(np.float32))
        mask = torch.nn.functional.one_hot(mask.long(), num_classes = config.num_classes)
        mask = mask.to(torch.float32)
        mask = mask.permute(2, 0, 1)

        return X.float(), mask
```

FIGURE 8.5   The "DroneSegmentationDataset" class and "__init__", "__len__", "__getitem__" methods.

One-hot encoding represents each pixel's class in a way that the model can better differentiate between classes using a multi-dimensional array. This type of encoding is very effective in model training during multi-class image segmentation. The first part of the "DroneSegmentationDataset" class is given in Figure 8.5.

A method called "read_images" is created to read, normalize, and rescale images. It reads images from the path defined by "config.Image_ PATH" and converts the color channel from BGR to RGB. These images are normalized (divided by 255), resized into default image weight/height as defined by default configurations, and transformed along with bound box dimensions (Figure 8.6).

In order to increase the number of training images, an image augmentation technique is applied. The image augmentation generally improves the model performance as it increases the original number of images available in the dataset. We have used the "augmentor" method to rotate images 90, 180, and 270 degrees, shear by −16 to 16 degrees, and apply flip operations to 50% of the images. These operations are done in random order (one of the operations is selected randomly each time) by setting the "random_order" to "True" as shown in Figure 8.6. The "SegmentationMapsOnImage" is used to create objects from masks for representing segmentation map associated with an image. The "get_arr()" function is used to get the segmentation map array with the original data type and shape.

```
def read_images(self,index):
    row = self.image_df.iloc[index]
    filename = str(config.data_dir+'/'+config.Image_PATH+row.filename) + '.jpg'
    image = cv2.imread(filename)
    image = cv2.cvtColor(image, cv2.COLOR_BGR2RGB)
    image = image/255.0
    image = cv2.resize(image,(config.img_width,config.img_height))
    return image

def read_masks(self,index):
    row = self.image_df.iloc[index]
    filename = str(config.data_dir+'/'+config.Mask_PATH+row.filename) + '.png'
    mask = cv2.imread(filename,cv2.IMREAD_GRAYSCALE)
    mask = cv2.resize(mask,(config.img_width,config.img_height))
    return mask

def augmentor(self,image,mask):
    seq = iaa.Sequential([
        iaa.OneOf([
            iaa.Affine(rotate=90),
            iaa.Affine(rotate=180),
            iaa.Affine(rotate=270),
            iaa.Affine(shear=(-16, 16)),
            iaa.Fliplr(0.5),
        ])], random_order=True)
    segmap = SegmentationMapsOnImage(mask, shape=image.shape)
    image_aug,mask_aug = seq(image=image, segmentation_maps=segmap)
    mask_aug = mask_aug.get_arr()
    return image_aug,mask_aug
```

FIGURE 8.6 "read_image", "read_masks", and "augmentor" methods to read and pre-process images and corresponding masks.

8.5 LOAD DATASET AND MODEL ARCHITECTURE

The "mean" and "std" variables are defined that are specific to the DeepLabV3_ResNet50 model. The training and validation dataset is prepared using the data lists, mean, and std by setting the mode to "trian" and "eval", respectively. Training images are also increased by implementing augmentations as defined by the "augmentor" method (Figure 8.6). The data loading utility of PyTorch, the "DataLoader" constructor is used with arguments for dataset ("train_gen"), batch size, shuffling, and pin memory. This constructor wraps an iterable around the defined dataset ("train_gen" or "val_gen") and facilitates easy access to the images. Detailed explanations of these arguments are explained in [9]. The validation testing is also done using the "DataLoader" but on the validation dataset without shuffling (Figure 8.7).

After the dataset is imported and pre-processed, the next step would be training and testing the deep learning network. At this stage, we need to import the packages required to run the DeepLabV3 model. The "optim" is imported to implement different optimization algorithms and the "torchvision" module is utilized to access various model architectures and weights

```
##DataLoader
from torch.utils.data import DataLoader

mean=[0.485, 0.456, 0.406]
std=[0.229, 0.224, 0.225]

model_path = f'{config.data_dir}'

train_gen = DroneSegmentationDataset(train_data_list,mean,std,augment=True,mode="train")
val_gen = DroneSegmentationDataset(valid_data_list,mean,std,augment=False,mode="eval")

train_loader = DataLoader(train_gen,batch_size=config.batch_size,shuffle=True,pin_memory=True)
val_loader = DataLoader(val_gen,batch_size=config.batch_size,shuffle=False,pin_memory=True)
```

FIGURE 8.7 Define model parameters and pre-process images using the "DataLoader" constructor to facilitate easy access to training and validation datasets.

[10]. The pre-trained model "deeplabv3_resnet50" is imported from "torch-vision.models.segmentation" with default weights. The model is also transformed for doing data manipulation, making it suitable for training. After loading the model, if we check it in the Spyder's console window (by entering "model"), it will return its internal architecture. There in the model classifier DeepLabhead expects 2048 input features, and in the model's aux classifier FCNHead expects 1024 input features. These feature numbers need to be changed for transfer learning. The model architecture ("model.classifier" and "model.aux_classifier") is updated to match the input features and the number of classes in our dataset (config.num_classes = 23). To run the model on multiple GPUs, data parallelism is used so that each of the smaller subsets of data can be processed independently by different GPUs (in our case, the number of GPUs = 2). If using a single GPU workstation, the "nn.DataParallel(model)" command needs to be commented out or deleted. After these pre-processing operations, the model is moved to CUDA using the "model.cuda()" command (Figure 8.8).

Next, we implement the focal loss function that adds a factor to the standard cross-entropy loss to down-weights the losses and gives more

```
# model
from torch import nn,optim
from torchvision.models.segmentation import deeplabv3_resnet50, DeepLabV3_ResNet50_Weights
from torchvision.models.segmentation.deeplabv3 import DeepLabHead
from torchvision.models.segmentation.fcn import FCNHead

model = deeplabv3_resnet50(weights=DeepLabV3_ResNet50_Weights.DEFAULT)
model.classifier = DeepLabHead(2048, config.num_classes)
model.aux_classifier = FCNHead(1024, config.num_classes)

model= nn.DataParallel(model)
model= model.cuda()
```

FIGURE 8.8 Setting up the imported model for transfer learning by changing its classifier, using data parallelism, and moving the model to CUDA for GPU processing.

```
#Loss Function
#Focal Loss
ALPHA = 0.8
GAMMA = 2
class FocalLoss(nn.Module):
    def __init__(self, weight=None, size_average=True):
        super(FocalLoss, self).__init__()

    def forward(self, inputs, targets, alpha=ALPHA, gamma=GAMMA, smooth=1):

        #remove it if model contains a sigmoid or equivalent activation layer
        inputs = torch.sigmoid(inputs)

        #flatten label and prediction tensors
        inputs = inputs.view(-1)
        targets = targets.view(-1)

        #compute binary cross-entropy for focal loss calculatoin
        BCE = torch.nn.functional.binary_cross_entropy(inputs, targets, reduction='mean')
        BCE_EXP = torch.exp(-BCE)
        focal_loss = alpha * (1-BCE_EXP)**gamma * BCE

        return focal_loss

criterion = FocalLoss().cuda()
```

FIGURE 8.9 Focal loss function for dealing with class imbalance by downweighting the losses.

importance to the harder or misclassified examples than easily or correctly classified ones [11]. Although it was initially developed for object detection tasks, it can effectively be used for semantic segmentations or sequence classification tasks using RNNs. The focal loss function used in this case study is shown in Figure 8.9. The focal loss equation uses ALPHA and GAMMA constants to adjust the rate for downweighting easily classified examples.

The Adam optimizer is defined using model parameters, learning rate, and weight decay. The "StepLR" scheduler is used with 5 five-step size and a multiplicative factor of 0.5 to reduce the learning rate by half after five epochs. Finally, the "requires_grad" is set to True for automatic differentiation or "autograd" recording operation (Figure 8.10). However, this can be set to False to check model performance.

It is recommended to launch Spyder IDE from "Anaconda Prompt" by entering the command "spyder" and running each of the program sections

```
#optimizer and scheduler
optimizer = optim.Adam(model.parameters(),lr =config.lr,weight_decay = 0.001)
scheduler = optim.lr_scheduler.StepLR(optimizer,step_size=5,gamma=0.5)

### requires gradient (True) can be used for fine-tuning the model.
for param in model.parameters():
    param.requires_grad = True
```

FIGURE 8.10 Defining optimizer and scheduler parameters for model training.

separately or line by line. For example, to run a section of the program in Spyder IDE (Windows), we may select multiple lines of code and press the "F9" button. This process will help the user to understand the codes step-by-step and pinpoint an error quickly. This case study example uses two GPUs (GeForce RTX 3090) with data parallelism to split the batches.

8.6 MODEL TRAINING AND SAVING THE BEST MODEL

Now the model is ready for training. A nested "for loop" is used to run the training for a number of epochs set by the default configurations ("config.epochs"). In this case study, the model is going to run for 15 epochs. Figure 8.11 shows the code for training the model on multiple CUDAs and calculating loss in every iteration. A "step_check" variable is created to check and save the best model four times in an epoch. Initially, the best loss is set to a very large number (np.inf), and after every iteration, the program updates this best loss if a lower loss value is found. For this semantic segmentation problem, total training loss is the summation of all losses defined by criterion in Figure 8.9 (i.e., focal loss function). The "torch.cuda. empty_cache()" is used before training to release all unoccupied cashed memory for effective GPU operation. The code for this training process and printing the epoch numbers, training loss, and validation loss are shown in Figure 8.11.

The model training may return the "OutOfMemoryError: CUDA out of memory" error, which is an issue of GPU memory limitations. In that situation, the code won't execute, but the user can resolve this problem by reducing the batch size or image size. Sometimes, restarting the kernel in the Spyder console may solve the out-of-memory issue.

Once the model runs and starts to train, we get a minimum validation loss of 0.00447 after 15 epochs (Figure 8.12). In this case study, the training and validation datasets are randomly splitted, where the allocated training and validation images are 80% and 20% of the total images, respectively. In some machine learning practices, the total dataset is divided into three different categories: training, validation, and testing. Although both validation and testing datasets can be used interchangeably, in some cases, for unbiased evaluation of the model, the validation dataset may be utilized for early stopping in overfitting scenarios [12]. During training, if we find the best training loss within the first one or two epochs and after that loss increases randomly, the training should be terminated as it indicates that the model is failing to generalize the dataset and is overfitting.

```python
#training
step_check = len(train_loader)/4
steps = 0
best_loss= np.inf
torch.cuda.empty_cache()
for epoch in range(config.epochs):
    model.train()
    train_losses = 0

    for images, masks in iter(train_loader):
        images, masks = images.cuda(), masks.cuda()
        steps += 1
        output = model(images)

        loss = criterion(output['out'], masks)
        optimizer.zero_grad()
        loss.backward()
        optimizer.step()

        train_losses += loss.item()
        if steps % step_check == 0:
            model.eval()
            val_losses = 0
            with torch.no_grad():
                for images, masks in iter(val_loader):
                    images, masks = images.cuda(), masks.cuda()
                    output = model(images)
                    loss = criterion(output['out'], masks)
                    val_losses += loss.item()

            if val_losses < best_loss:
                best_loss = val_losses
                print('saving model...')
                torch.save(model, model_path+'/model.pt')

            print("Epoch: {}/{}.. ".format(epoch+1, config.epochs),
                  "Training Loss: {:.5f}.. ".format(train_losses),
                  "Validation Loss: {:.5f}.. ".format(val_losses),
                  )
            train_losses = 0
            model.train()
    scheduler.step()
print('Finish!')
```

FIGURE 8.11 Model training and saving the best model, and printing training and validation losses.

```
Epoch: 13/15..  Training Loss: 0.00445..  Validation Loss: 0.00543..
saving model...
Epoch: 13/15..  Training Loss: 0.00453..  Validation Loss: 0.00489..
Epoch: 14/15..  Training Loss: 0.00445..  Validation Loss: 0.00520..
Epoch: 14/15..  Training Loss: 0.00387..  Validation Loss: 0.00535..
Epoch: 14/15..  Training Loss: 0.00391..  Validation Loss: 0.00587..
Epoch: 14/15..  Training Loss: 0.00399..  Validation Loss: 0.00501..
Epoch: 15/15..  Training Loss: 0.00385..  Validation Loss: 0.00496..
saving model...
Epoch: 15/15..  Training Loss: 0.00396..  Validation Loss: 0.00447..
Epoch: 15/15..  Training Loss: 0.00403..  Validation Loss: 0.00475..
Epoch: 15/15..  Training Loss: 0.00386..  Validation Loss: 0.00484..
Finish!
```

FIGURE 8.12   Best "Training Loss" is 0.00396 and "Validation Loss" is 0.00447 after running the model for 15 epochs.

8.7 MODEL TESTING AND INFERENCE

We may test the model performance by segmenting drone images from the dataset manually. Figures 8.13 and 8.14 show the code required to load the trained model from "model_path", create a custom function to plot segmented maps, and process images for segmentation using a function called "process_image". The "process_image" function takes a raw image and trained model as inputs and returns the raw image, segmented image by the model, and an image showing the segmented image overlayed on the raw image to see the differences.

In the "process_image" function, the "pyplot" library from "matplotlib" is used for displaying the images (Figure 8.14). The raw image is processed similarly to the model inputs during training. The image color channels are converted from BGR to RGB since the order of colors in OpenCV is BGR. The image is then resized, normalized, transformed, and unsqueezed

```
#load the saved model
model =  torch.load(model_path+'/model.pt')
model = model.cuda()
model.eval();

################
#create custom function to plot segmented maps
meta_df = pd.read_csv(f'{config.data_dir}/archive/class_dict_seg.csv')
label_to_name = {t:d['name'] for t,d in meta_df.iterrows()}
name_to_label = {v:k for k,v in label_to_name.items()}
label_to_bgr = {t:(d[' b'],d[' g'],d[' r']) for t,d in meta_df.iterrows()}
```

FIGURE 8.13   Load the trained model from "model_path" and create a custom function to plot segmented maps.

```python
import matplotlib.pyplot as plt
def process_image(raw_image,model):
    image = cv2.cvtColor(raw_image, cv2.COLOR_BGR2RGB)
    image = cv2.resize(image,(config.img_width,config.img_height))
    image = image/255.0
    image = T.Compose([T.ToTensor(), T.Normalize(mean, std)])(image.copy())
    image = image.unsqueeze(0)
    image = image.float().cuda()
    output = model(image)["out"][0].cpu()
    label = torch.argmax(output, dim=0).numpy()
    ####
    red_ch   = np.zeros_like(label).astype(np.uint8)
    green_ch = np.zeros_like(label).astype(np.uint8)
    blue_ch  = np.zeros_like(label).astype(np.uint8)
    for label_num in range(0, len(label_to_bgr)):
        index = label == label_num
        B,G,R = label_to_bgr[label_num]
        red_ch[index]   = R
        green_ch[index] = G
        blue_ch[index]  = B
    segmented_map = np.stack([red_ch, green_ch, blue_ch], axis=2)
    width,height,_ = raw_image.shape
    segmented_image = cv2.resize(segmented_map, (height,width ))
    #####
    alpha = 1   # transparency for the original image
    beta  = 0.4 # transparency for the segmentation map
    gamma = 0
    image = np.array(raw_image)
    image = cv2.cvtColor(image, cv2.COLOR_RGB2BGR)
    segmented_image = cv2.cvtColor(segmented_image, cv2.COLOR_RGB2BGR)
    overlay_image = cv2.addWeighted(image, alpha, segmented_image, beta, gamma, image)
    ####
    #plot the figures
    plt.figure(figsize=(12, 10), dpi=100)
    plt.subplot(1, 3, 1)
    plt.axis("off")
    plt.title("Image")
    plt.imshow(np.asarray(raw_image))
    plt.subplot(1, 3, 2)
    plt.title("Segmentation")
    plt.axis("off")
    plt.imshow(segmented_image)

    plt.subplot(1, 3, 3)
    plt.title("Overlayed")
    plt.axis("off")
    plt.imshow(overlay_image[:, :, ::-1])
    plt.show()
    plt.close()
```

FIGURE 8.14 The "process_image" function to process the image through the trained model and plot the original, segmented, and overlayed images.

to load into CUDA. The output segmented image is determined by a variable called "output". The "torch.argmax" is used to get labels or indices of the maximum value of all elements. The segmented image is created by stacking data from red, green, and blue channels and by resizing the segmented map. Here, "alpha" and "beta" are constants that define the overlay

```
raw_image = cv2.imread(config.data_dir+'/'+config.Image_PATH + "281.jpg")
process_image(raw_image,model)
```

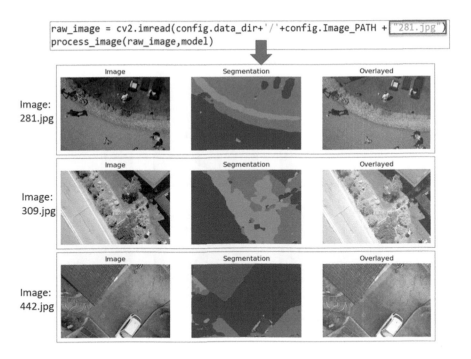

FIGURE 8.15   Raw, segmented, and overlayed images. Here, the segmented image is generated using the trained model.

transparency of the original and segmented images, respectively. Finally, three figures can be plotted as shown in Figure 8.15 to compare actual and segmented images.

After defining the "process_image" function for model testing, different images from the validation dataset are loaded and tested. The results of testing three different images (281.jpg, 309.jpg, and 442.jpg) are given in Figure 8.15.

Now we can make the model inference using entirely new images in the real-world context. To test this, three different open-source pictures are downloaded from https://unsplash.com/. These pictures are renamed (e.g., Test1.jpg, Test2.jpg, and Test3.jpg) and available in the additional resources of this chapter. In our workstation, the images are saved into the folder defined by "config.data_dir" as shown in Figure 8.16. The inference images are processed and plotted using the "process_image" function. We can see that the model can segment these images to some degree. Roads and trees can be easily detected by the model. Typically, a trained model can predict with a higher confidence level if the image features and

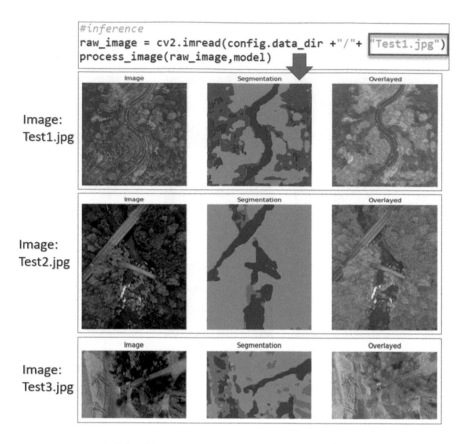

FIGURE 8.16   Model inference using test images downloaded from online.

outlooks are similar to the dataset images. For a practical implementation case, a dataset can be created for model training so that the model sees a similar variation of pictures during training.

8.7.1 Fine Tuning

For finding the optimal set of parameters for the best learning process, it is recommended to tweak different parameters and evaluate the outputs that minimize the loss and improve training/inference time. The codes given for this chapter can be updated by changing batch size, epochs, learning rate, optimizer, schedulers, etc. To understand the effect of different hyperparameters on the model tuning, please refer to Sections 6.9.1 and 6.9.2 from Chapter 6. The exercise section of Chapter 6 also discusses the effect of using different hyperparameters. We may also use other pretrained models for model training, as shown in Chapter 7. In this chapter, we focus on the effect of using various loss functions.

8.7.2 Using a Different Loss Function

This case study uses a loss function called focal loss. Other common types of loss functions for segmentation tasks are Binary Cross-Entropy (BCE), Categorical Cross-Entropy (CCE), Dice, and Intersection over Union (IoU) Losses. The program presented in this chapter can be used for other loss functions just by replacing the loss function defined in Figure 8.9. We may also create a customized loss function by adding various losses and assigning different weights to different losses. For example, if we want to use a loss that is a combination of Dice and BCE loss, only the loss function section in Figure 8.9 needs to be updated as shown in Figure 8.17. The Dice loss is typically used for measuring the overlaps between predicted segmentation and the original images. On the other hand, BCE loss is used during binary segmentation tasks where each pixel is classified as either foreground or background.

Using "DiceBCELoss", we find the best validation loss of 0.93385 after 15 epochs (Figure 8.18). This number is not comparable to the best loss found using focal loss as they have different rules for finding losses. To evaluate the model performance using "DiceBCELoss" we may check the segmented and overlayed images by the trained model.

To compare the performance difference between focal loss and "DiceBCELoss" we test similar images that were shown in Figure 8.15. These segmentations and overlayed images are shown in Figure 8.19. By comparing the segmented images from Figure 8.15 and 8.19, we can

```
#Loss Function
#Dice BCE Loss
import torch.nn.functional as F

class DiceBCELoss(nn.Module):
    def __init__(self, weight=None, size_average=True):
        super(DiceBCELoss, self).__init__()

    def forward(self, inputs, targets, smooth=1):

        #comment out if your model contains a sigmoid or equivalent activation layer
        inputs = F.sigmoid(inputs)

        #flatten label and prediction tensors
        inputs = inputs.view(-1)
        targets = targets.view(-1)

        intersection = (inputs * targets).sum()
        dice_loss = 1 - (2.*intersection + smooth)/(inputs.sum() + targets.sum() + smooth)
        BCE = F.binary_cross_entropy(inputs, targets, reduction='mean')
        Dice_BCE = BCE + dice_loss

        return Dice_BCE

criterion = DiceBCELoss().cuda()
```

FIGURE 8.17   Using Dice and BCE loss as a loss function.

```
Epoch: 14/15..  Training Loss: 0.96253..  Validation Loss: 0.96734..
Epoch: 14/15..  Training Loss: 0.89079..  Validation Loss: 0.99414..
Epoch: 14/15..  Training Loss: 0.95135..  Validation Loss: 0.99732..
Epoch: 15/15..  Training Loss: 0.94546..  Validation Loss: 0.98816..
saving model...
Epoch: 15/15..  Training Loss: 0.89648..  Validation Loss: 0.96334..
saving model...
Epoch: 15/15..  Training Loss: 0.90722..  Validation Loss: 0.94611..
saving model...
Epoch: 15/15..  Training Loss: 0.90335..  Validation Loss: 0.93385..
Finish!
```

FIGURE 8.18 "Training Loss" is 0.90335 and "Validation Loss" is 0.93385 after running the model for 15 epochs.

conclude that Dice BCE loss returns better performance in this case. In the image "281.jpg", the model can segment people to some degree in the Dice BCE case. However, using a different loss is just an example, and the performance of the model can be improved by increasing epochs and other hypermeters.

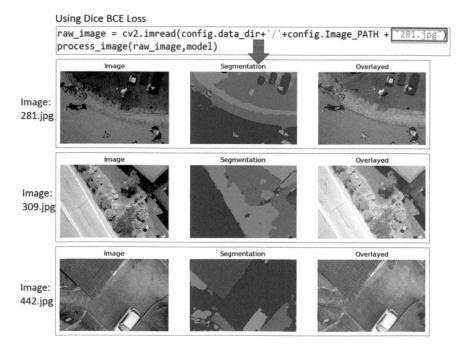

FIGURE 8.19 Raw, segmented, and overlayed images. Here the segmented image is generated using the trained model where the Dice BCE loss function is used instead of focal loss.

Using Dice BCE Loss

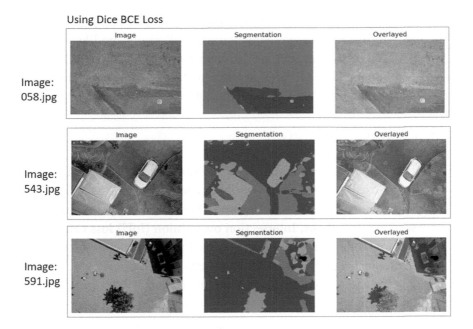

FIGURE 8.20   Raw, segmented, and overlaid images for 058.jpg, 543.jpg, and 591. jpg images when the Dice BCE loss function is used.

A few other random images are also segmented using the Dice BCE loss model. These segmented and overlayed images are shown in Figure 8.20.

8.8 SIMILAR APPLICATIONS FOR ENGINEERS

This chapter presents a case study of the image segmentation problem using deep learning. The image dataset used here is freely available on Kaggel's site, and it is highly recommended that readers of this book try running the model using the same dataset. In the engineering fields, image segmentation has numerous practical applications. For example, in autonomous driving, image segmentation is widely used for scene understanding and for identifying pixel areas for pedestrians, traffic signals, and road curbs. It is a critical technology for enabling safe driving in autonomous cars. In robotics, image segmentation is used for object recognition and safe manipulations. In the medical field, this technology is very critical for organ segmentation, cell counting, and anomaly detection. Besides these common tasks, the use of image segmentation is rapidly growing in document checking, Augmented Reality (AR) applications, video surveillance, crop or plant growth monitoring, quality controls in supply chains, satellite image analysis, and many more. Current technological trends suggest that practical image segmentation applications are likely to grow in many engineering fields in the coming years.

The following section presents segmentation model programming questions related to using different types of loss functions.

8.9 EXERCISE PROBLEM

1. In this chapter, a semantic segmentation drone dataset from Kaggle's site is used for segmenting aerial images. The case study shows the implementations of focal loss and DiceBCE loss in the model. For segmentation tasks, Intersection over Union (IoU) loss can be used as a loss function as well [13], and the PyTorch function required for implementing different loss functions is available at ref. [14]. Use IoU loss instead of focal loss for this segmentation model and comment on the model performance after 15 epochs.

2. The Lovaz loss function is another effective function that can be used for semantic segmentation tasks [15]. The function required for implementing different Lovaz loss is available at GitHub [16]. Download the Lovaz loss function from the GitHub page and implement Lovaz softmax loss in the case study model. Run the model for 15 epochs and comment on the model performance.

REFERENCES

1. Chen, L.-C., Papandreou, G., Schroff, F., and Adam, H., 2017, "Rethinking Atrous Convolution for Semantic Image Segmentation.", https://arxiv.org/abs/1706.05587.
2. GHINASSI, A., 2023, "Semantic Segmentation Drone Dataset," https://www.kaggle.com/datasets/santurini/semantic-segmentation-drone-dataset.
3. Soumith Chintala, G. C., Dzhulgakov, D., Yang, E., and Shulga, N., 2023, "PyTorch," https://github.com/pytorch/pytorch.
4. PyTorch, 2023, "Transforming and augmenting images," https://pytorch.org/vision/stable/transforms.html.
5. Bradski, G., 2000, "The openCV Library," Dr," Dobb's Journal: Software Tools for the Professional Programmer, 25(11), pp. 120–123.
6. imgaug, 2020, "Overview of augmenters.", https://imgaug.readthedocs.io/en/latest/source/overview_of_augmenters.html.
7. 2020, "imgaug.augmentables.segmaps," https://imgaug.readthedocs.io/en/latest/source/api_augmentables_segmaps.html.

8. 2023, "Transforming and augmenting images," https://pytorch.org/vision/stable/transforms.html#torchvision.transforms.ToTensor.

9. 2023, "Torch.utils.data," https://pytorch.org/docs/stable/data.html.

10. 2023, "PyTorch torch.optim," https://pytorch.org/docs/stable/optim.html.

11. Lin, T.-Y., Goyal, P., Girshick, R., He, K., and Dollar, P., 2017, "Focal Loss for Dense Object Detection," 2017 IEEE International Conference on Computer Vision (ICCV), IEEE Computer Society, pp. 2999–3007.

12. Prechelt, L., 2012, "Early Stopping—But When?," Neural Networks: Tricks of the Trade: 2nd Ed., G. Montavon, G. B. Orr, and K.-R. Müller, eds., Springer, Berlin Heidelberg, pp. 53–67.

13. Girshick, R., Donahue, J., Darrell, T., and Malik, J., 2013, "Rich Feature Hierarchies for Accurate Object Detection and Semantic Segmentation," Proceedings of the IEEE Computer Society Conference on Computer Vision and Pattern Recognition, pp. 580–587.

14. RNA, 2021, "Loss Function Library - Keras & PyTorch," https://www.kaggle.com/code/bigironsphere/loss-function-library-keras-pytorch.

15. Berman, M., Rannen, A., and Blaschko, M., 2018, The Lovasz-Softmax Loss: A Tractable Surrogate for the Optimization of the Intersection-Over-Union Measure in Neural Networks., https://arxiv.org/abs/1705.08790

16. Berman, M., 2019, "The Lovász-Softmax loss: A tractable surrogate for the optimization of the intersection-over-union measure in neural networks," https://github.com/bermanmaxim/LovaszSoftmax.

## CHAPTER 9

Case Study IV

Image Captioning

9.1 PROBLEM STATEMENT

Case Study IV demonstrates a practical implementation of deep learning for image captioning problems. In this case study, we have used the ResNet50 model with Long Short-Term Memory (LSTM) network to generate a textual description of an image using deep learning. The LSTM is a type of RNN that is capable of processing sequences of texts, speech, or videos. It is widely used to model sequence data in natural language processing, audio/video analysis, sentiment analysis, etc. To train and test our model, an open-source dataset called "Flickr 8k Dataset" is used. The dataset has 8091 images and corresponding captions. Each of the images has five different captions that provide a clear description of salient entities and events. This dataset can be downloaded from Kaggle's site [1]. The "Images" folder inside "flickr8k" has all the images in .jpg format, and the "caption.txt" file has all the captions. Our goal in this case study is to train a deep-learning model using CNN and RNN so that it can generate captions from pictures based on trained knowledge. We recommend readers of this book download the dataset and reproduce the results by following the instructions given in Chapter 5 (for GPU setup) and executing the codes given in this chapter.

A schematic of the learning process using CNN and LSTM is shown in Figure 9.1. In this case study, we have used an attention mechanism algorithm that allows the model to focus on different locations of the image during

DOI: 10.1201/9781003402923-9

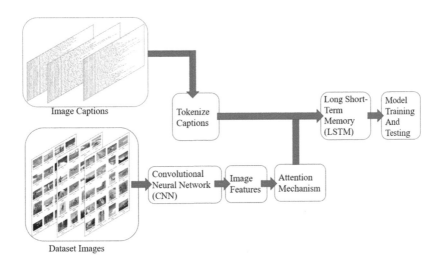

FIGURE 9.1 Schematic of using CNN and LSTM architectures for image captioning tasks.

training. First, the images are processed through CNN to generate features that go through the attention mechanism to provide different weights to highlight different feature vectors. It is then passed through the LSTM with the tokenized captions for training. After successful training and testing on the data set, we used several random images (downloaded from online) to evaluate the performance of the model by generating meaningful captions of unseen images. Figure 9.1 presents a schematic of applying CNN and RNN (LSTM) architectures for image captioning tasks.

In the following sections, Python codes for the training and testing operations are explained. All of the codes presented in this chapter are written and executed using Spyder Integrated Developed Environment (IDE) from Anaconda. It is important to note that Spyder IDE should be launched using Anaconda Navigator or by executing the "spyder" command in "Anaconda Prompt". Otherwise, the program may not find the required CUDA environment for PyTorch, and the "torch.cuda.is_available()" command in Spyder's console will return "False".

9.2 DEFINING DEFAULT CONFIGURATION

Our first task is to create Python classes that can group similar types of data and functions. The "Class" in Python forms an object to maintain a set of attributes. Here, in this program, a new class variable (DefaultConfigs) is created to set or define important default parameters (objects) that can be

```
class DefaultConfigs(object):
    data_dir = r"C:\Users\tariqarif\Desktop\Image_Captioning\archive"
    Image_PATH = '/flickr8k/images/'
    img_width = 512
    img_height = 512
    channels = 3
    lr = 0.001
    batch_size = 32
    epochs = 15
    seed= 12

config = DefaultConfigs()
```

FIGURE 9.2   Create a "DefaultConfigs" class to define parameters that will be used throughout the program.

used throughout the program. The "DefaultConfigs" class is called using a variable named "config" (Figure 9.2), and all of the class attributes can be accessed using the reference operator dot, ".". Here, declared class objects "data_dir" and "Image_PATH" are defined to assign data locations of the "Images" folder and caption text. The "img_width", "img_height", "channels", "lr" (learning rate), "batch_size", "epochs", and, "seed" are defined to assign default numerical values.

9.3 RANDOM SEED AND IMPORT MODULES/LIBRARIES

In this section, major modules and libraries required for running a deep-learning model for image captioning are presented. First, we import Python's "random", "numpy", and "torch" libraries. Then a function "set_all_random_seed" is defined to set random seeds of "numpy" and "torch" using the default seed assigned in Figure 9.2. Figure 9.3 shows the commands in Spyder editor for importing these libraries and the function.

```
import random
import numpy as np
import torch

def set_all_random_seed(seed = config.seed):
    random.seed(seed)
    np.random.seed(seed)
    torch.manual_seed(seed)
    torch.cuda.manual_seed_all(seed)
    return seed
print(f'random seed {set_all_random_seed()}')
```

FIGURE 9.3   Import the "random", "numpy", and "torch" libraries and define "set_all_random_seed" function.

```
import pandas as pd
caption_df = pd.read_csv(f'{config.data_dir}'+"/flickr8k/captions.csv")

###take one random caption per image
image_ids = [i for i in caption_df['image'].unique()]
captions = []
for i in image_ids:
    captions.append(caption_df.loc[caption_df['image']==i]['caption'].iloc[random.randint(0, 4)])
df = pd.DataFrame({'image':image_ids,'caption':captions})

##############
from sklearn.model_selection import train_test_split
train_data_list,valid_data_list = train_test_split(df,test_size = 0.2,random_state = config.seed+1)
```

FIGURE 9.4   Import "pandas" and create a data frame to take one random caption for an image. Also, import "train_test_split" to split the train and validation data list.

To read the data from the dataset and to create a data frame, the "pandas" library is imported. In the dataset, each image has five different captions in a text file. We convert this text file into a ".csv" file. This can be done by just dragging and dropping the captions.txt file on an empty spreadsheet (Excel), and then selecting the "Text to Columns" options from the "Data" tab. There will be an option to select "Delimited" and press "Next" to select "Tab" and "Comma" delimiters to separate out these data (Image name and Captions) into two columns. Then save the file as ".csv" format (e.g., captions.csv) that has separate columns for the image name and corresponding captions. In this example, we want to pre-process the data in such a way that during training, the algorithm takes one of the five captions randomly for an image. Figure 9.4 shows the Python code for creating a data frame using an image list and one of the random captions from the "captions.csv" file.

The "sklearn.model_selection" class is used to pre-process data for training. All data were randomly divided into training and testing datasets using the "train_test_split()" method. Figure 9.4 shows the training images are split where the test data size is 20% of the total training data. An integer (config.seed+1) 13 is assigned to "random_state" so that the code can reproduce similar outputs later.

9.4 TOKENIZE CAPTIONS

For the natural language process, we need to break down the caption words into manageable units called tokens. Most of the deep learning models that are used for text analysis require the tokenized version of words, where each word is assigned to a numerical value instead of raw letters. It helps the model to learn efficiently by reducing the dimensionality of the inputs. In the English language, typically, combinations of letters construct a meaningful

```
##Libraries to tokenize word
caption = caption_df.iloc[0].caption
#NLTK
import nltk
nltk.download('punkt')  #only for the first time
tokens_nltk = nltk.tokenize.word_tokenize(str(caption).lower())

#####################
##Create vocabulary (i.e., dictionary of all words) for the dataset
from collections import Counter
counter = Counter()
for i in range(len(caption_df)):
    caption = str(caption_df.iloc[i].caption)
    tokens = nltk.tokenize.word_tokenize(caption.lower())
    counter.update(tokens)

threshold = 2 # if the word frequency is less than 'threshold', then the word is discarded.
words = [word for word, cnt in counter.items() if cnt >= threshold]
```

FIGURE 9.5   Import NLTK library for tokenization of words.

word. So tokenization can be done at the word level in the text input, where they are separated by spaces. In this case study, we have used the natural language toolkit (NLTK) library to tokenize words for model training [2]. NLTK provides easy-to-use interfaces to many lexical resources and suites for text-processing libraries. Figure 9.5 shows how the NLTK is imported to convert words into lower cases and to assign caption text data into different tokens. The "nltk.download('puntk')" command needs to run only once for the first time. Once it is downloaded, we should comment out that line. The "counter" module form "collections" is utilized to count the appearance of each word in the token. Here, a threshold variable is used to drop out any of the captions that are equal to or less than two words.

Now, a class called "Vocabulary" is used to create two dictionaries, one for words and one for corresponding indices. Repeated words and indices won't be added to the dictionaries. A vocabulary wrapper adds four unique tokens '<pads>', '<start>', '<end>', and '<unk>' for defining '0', '1', '2', and '3' indices, respectively (Figure 9.6). So each of the captions will start with the '<start>' index and will end with the '<end>' index. In the captions, we have found a total of 4669 words (including unique tokens) that construct the vocabulary dictionary for the training process.

9.5 DEFINE DATASET CLASS AND ATTRIBUTES

The "Dataset" library is imported for maintaining the data set effectively during the training process, "transform" is imported for transforming images [3], "cv2" is imported for reading image files [4], and "augmenters" is imported for implementing image augmentation sequences such as crop, horizontal/vertical flips, pooling [5]. The commands for importing these libraries and modules are shown in Figure 9.7.

```
##Vocabulary wrapper to create the dictionary
class Vocabulary(object):
    def __init__(self):
        self.word2idx = {}
        self.idx2word = {}
        self.idx = 0

    def add_word(self, word):
        if not word in self.word2idx:
            self.word2idx[word] = self.idx
            self.idx2word[self.idx] = word
            self.idx += 1

    def __len__(self):
        return len(self.word2idx)
# Create a vocab wrapper and add some special tokens.
vocab = Vocabulary()
vocab.add_word('<pad>')
vocab.add_word('<start>')
vocab.add_word('<end>')
vocab.add_word('<unk>')
# Add the words to the vocabulary.
for i, word in enumerate(words):
    vocab.add_word(word)
```

FIGURE 9.6 Create a vocabulary dictionary for words and indices, and assign unique tokens for "<pads>", "<start>", "<end>", and "<unk>".

A new class variable called "ImageCaptionDataset" is defined that has five different attributes. These are "images_df", "augment", "mode", "mean", and "std". These attribute assignments are shown in Figure 9.8. The "__init__" method is used for setting up the initial value of the instance, and the "__len__" method returns the number of image items in the image

```
#Dataset
from torch.utils.data import Dataset
from torchvision import transforms as T
import cv2
from imgaug import augmenters as iaa
```

FIGURE 9.7 Importing "Dataset", "transforms", "cv2", and "augmenters" for data processing.

```
class ImageCaptionDataset(Dataset):
    def __init__(self,images_df,mean,std,augment=True,mode="train"):

        self.image_df = images_df.copy()
        self.augment = augment
        self.mode = mode
        self.mean = mean
        self.std = std

    def __len__(self):
        return len(self.image_df)

    def __getitem__(self,index):
        X = self.read_images(index)
        y = self.image_df.iloc[index].caption

        if self.augment:
            X = self.augmentor(X)

        X = T.Compose([T.ToTensor(), T.Normalize(self.mean, self.std)])(X.copy())
        tokens = nltk.tokenize.word_tokenize(str(y).lower())
        caption = []
        caption.append(vocab.word2idx['<start>'])
        caption.extend([vocab.word2idx[token] if token in vocab.word2idx else vocab.word2idx['<unk>'] for token in tokens])
        caption.append(vocab.word2idx['<end>'])
        target = torch.LongTensor(caption)
        return X.float(), target
```

FIGURE 9.8   The "ImageCaptionDataset" class and "__init__", "__len__", "__getitem__" methods.

data frame, and the "__getitem__" method reads images and corresponding indices. The "augmentor()" method is utilized by "__getitem__" to aid the artificial image generations. "__getitem__" also uses "ToTensor()" to convert the "ndarray" (image features) to tensors and scale pixel intensity values from 0 to 1 [6]. The method converts the captions into lowercase and then creates tokens. These tokens are added to a list called "caption" which starts with '<start>' (i.e., 1), followed by tokens for captions, and ends with '<end>' (i.e., 2). If tokens are not found for the validation data, it will assign '<unk>' (i.e., 3 for unknown). The '<pad>' token is used for padding, which standardizes the length of sequences of words in a batch. The first part of the "ImageCaptionDataset" class is given in Figure 9.8.

A method called "read_images" is created to read, normalize, and rescale images. It reads images from the path defined by "config.Image_PATH" and converts the color channel from BGR to RGB. These images are normalized (divided by 255) and resized into default image weight/height as defined by default configurations (Figure 9.9).

In order to increase the number of training images, an image augmentation technique is applied. The image augmentation generally improves the model performance as it increases the original number of images available in the dataset. We have used the "augmentor" method to rotate images 90, 180, and 270 degrees, shear by −16 to 16 degrees, and apply flip operations to 50% of the images. These operations are done in random order (one of the operations is selected randomly each time) by setting the "random_order" to "True" as shown in Figure 9.9.

```
def read_images(self,index):
    row = self.image_df.iloc[index]
    filename = config.data_dir + config.Image_PATH + str(row.image)
    image = cv2.imread(filename)
    image = cv2.cvtColor(image, cv2.COLOR_BGR2RGB)
    image = image/255.0
    image = cv2.resize(image,(config.img_width,config.img_height))
    return image

def augmentor(self,image):
    seq = iaa.Sequential([
        iaa.OneOf([
            iaa.Affine(rotate=90),
            iaa.Affine(rotate=180),
            iaa.Affine(rotate=270),
            iaa.Affine(shear=(-16, 16)),
            iaa.Fliplr(0.5),

        ])], random_order=True)

    image_aug = seq.augment_image(image)
    return image_aug
```

FIGURE 9.9 "read_image" and "augmentor" methods to read and augment images for training.

9.6 LOAD DATASET AND MODEL ARCHITECTURE

The "pad_sequence" function from "nn.utils.rnn" is imported for using pad sequence operation. It pads shorter sequences with zeros to match the length of all sentences or captions. The data loading utility of PyTorch, the "DataLoader" constructor is used with arguments for dataset ("train_gen"), batch size, shuffling, pin memory, and collate function. The "Collate_FN" is created to properly stack all data in the data loader using padding values. This constructor wraps an iterable around the defined dataset ("train_gen" or "val_gen") and facilitates easy access to the images. Detailed explanations of these arguments are explained in [7]. The validation testing is also done using the "DataLoader" but on the validation dataset without shuffling (Figure 9.10).

After the dataset is imported and pre-processed, the next step would be training and testing the deep learning network. At this stage, we import the ResNet50 model with its default weights for CNN encoder operation, as shown in Figure 9.11. After importing the model, the "__init__" method of "EncoderCNN" drops the last two children (adaptive average pool and fully connected layers) from the network. Therefore, the features extracted

```
from torch.nn.utils.rnn import pad_sequence
from torch.utils.data import DataLoader

mean=[0.485, 0.456, 0.406]  #depends on the model
std=[0.229, 0.224, 0.225]   #depends on the model

class Collate_FN:
    def __init__(self,pad_id):
        self.pad_id = pad_id

    def __call__(self,batch):
        imgs = [item[0].unsqueeze(0) for item in batch]
        imgs = torch.cat(imgs,dim=0)

        targets = [item[1] for item in batch]
        target_lens = [len(target) for target in targets]
        targets = pad_sequence(targets, batch_first=True, padding_value=self.pad_id)
        return imgs,targets, target_lens

pad_id = vocab.word2idx["<pad>"]
train_gen = ImageCaptionDataset(train_data_list,mean,std,augment=True,mode="train")
train_loader = DataLoader(train_gen,batch_size=config.batch_size,shuffle=True,pin_memory=True,
                          collate_fn=Collate_FN(pad_id))

val_gen = ImageCaptionDataset(valid_data_list,mean,std,augment=False,mode="eval")
val_loader = DataLoader(val_gen,batch_size=config.batch_size,shuffle=False,pin_memory=True,
                        collate_fn=Collate_FN(pad_id))
```

FIGURE 9.10 Import "pad_seqence" and "Dataloader" to pre-process images with captions for training and validation.

through CNN architecture can be used for the LSTM network to train sequence data with images. After dropping these layers, the ResNet50 is passed through "nn.Sequential" to create another usable model.

9.6.1 Define Attention Mechanism

An attention mechanism is declared for the model so that it can focus on the dominant features of an image during the training process. Without

```
from torch import nn
import torchvision.models as models

class EncoderCNN(nn.Module):
    def __init__(self):
        super(EncoderCNN, self).__init__()
        resnet = models.resnet50(weights='DEFAULT')
        modules = list(resnet.children())[:-2]
        self.resnet = nn.Sequential(*modules)

    def forward(self, images):
        features = self.resnet(images)
        features = features.permute(0, 2, 3, 1)
        features = features.view(features.size(0), -1, features.size(-1))
        return features
```

FIGURE 9.11 Import "nn" from torch and "models" from "torchvision.models", and define the "EncoderCNN" class for modifying CNN architecture.

```
class Attention(nn.Module):
    def __init__(self, encoder_dim,decoder_dim,attention_dim):
        super(Attention, self).__init__()

        self.attention_dim = attention_dim

        self.U = nn.Linear(encoder_dim,attention_dim)
        self.W = nn.Linear(decoder_dim,attention_dim)
        self.A = nn.Linear(attention_dim,1)

    def forward(self, features, hidden_state):
        u_hs = self.U(features)
        w_ah = self.W(hidden_state)

        combined_states = torch.tanh(u_hs + w_ah.unsqueeze(1))

        attention_scores = self.A(combined_states)
        attention_scores = attention_scores.squeeze(2)

        alpha = torch.nn.functional.softmax(attention_scores,dim=1)

        attention_weights = features * alpha.unsqueeze(2)
        attention_weights = attention_weights.sum(dim=1)

        return alpha,attention_weights
```

FIGURE 9.12   Attention class and its methods (__init__ and forward) for generating attention weights.

the attention mechanism, the model will try to encode an entire input sequence into a vector and decode the output sequence at a time. This process might lead to loss of information or analyzing too much data. Therefore attention mechanism is implemented to focus on important features of the input sequence by assigning various levels of weights or attention scores and processing through RNN. The steps of RNN use this mechanism to determine important areas of an image and relate those for generating words one after another. The program for the "Attention" class and its methods (__init__ and forward) are shown in Figure 9.12. Here, the "__init__" method initiates linear layers and the "forward" method converts the encoder dimension to an attention dimension by passing the image features through the linear layer. The "hidden_state" in LSTM also goes through the attention after every step and generates attention scores accordingly.

The "DecoderRNN" class with "__init__", "forward", "init_ hidden_state", and "generate_caption" methods are defined (Figure 9.13). The "__init__" method initializes vocabulary size, attention dimension,

```
class DecoderRNN(nn.Module):
    def __init__(self,embed_size, vocab_size, attention_dim,encoder_dim,decoder_dim):
        super().__init__()

        self.vocab_size = vocab_size
        self.attention_dim = attention_dim
        self.decoder_dim = decoder_dim

        self.embedding = nn.Embedding(vocab_size,embed_size)
        self.attention = Attention(encoder_dim,decoder_dim,attention_dim)

        self.init_h = nn.Linear(encoder_dim, decoder_dim)
        self.init_c = nn.Linear(encoder_dim, decoder_dim)
        self.lstm_cell = nn.LSTMCell(embed_size+encoder_dim,decoder_dim,bias=True)
        self.f_beta = nn.Linear(decoder_dim, encoder_dim)

        self.fcn = nn.Linear(decoder_dim,vocab_size)
        self.drop = nn.Dropout(0.5)
```

FIGURE 9.13 "DecoderRNN" Class and "__init__" method for using LSTM cells.

and decoder dimension. Here, using the "forward" method (Figure 9.14), the attention dimension from the "Attention" class and word embedding are concatenated. Then they are passed through the LSTM cell to generate memory or forget unimportant features. The "nn.Linear" module is used to linearly transform the decoder dimension to vocabulary size, and the "nn.Dropout" module is used to implement dropout regularization and reduce overfitting.

The "init_hidden_state" method initializes hidden states of LSTM using mean encoder outputs. The "generate_caption" method passes the image features through attention to get context (attention-weighted features) which is then embedded with the "<start>" padding. This "<start>" and context then go through LSTM cells and a fully connected layer to get the output. The output word is embedded with subsequent context to produce a caption until the model predicts "<end>". Implementing these operations using Python methods is shown in Figure 9.14.

The "EncoderDecoder" class is created to combine the encoder and decoder into a single model. If they are not combined, the optimizer will require both the encoder and decoder parameters separately. This class has "__init__" and "forward" methods as shown in Figure 9.15.

The model is defined as "EncoderDecoder" and transferred to CUDA using "model().cuda()" as shown in Figure 9.16. To run the model on multiple GPUs, data parallelism is used so that each of the smaller subsets of data can be processed independently by different GPUs (in our case, number of GPUs = 2). If using a single GPU workstation, the "nn.DataParallel(model)" command needs to be commented out or deleted. The model passes the

```
def forward(self, features, captions):
    embeds = self.embedding(captions)
    h, c = self.init_hidden_state(features)
    seq_length = len(captions[0])-1
    batch_size = captions.size(0)
    preds = torch.zeros(batch_size, seq_length, self.vocab_size).cuda()
    for s in range(seq_length):
        _,context = self.attention(features, h)
        lstm_input = torch.cat((embeds[:, s], context), dim=1)
        output, _ = self.lstm_cell(lstm_input, (h, c))
        output = self.fcn(self.drop(output))
        preds[:,s] = output
    return preds

def init_hidden_state(self, encoder_out):
    mean_encoder_out = encoder_out.mean(dim=1)
    h = self.init_h(mean_encoder_out)
    c = self.init_c(mean_encoder_out)
    return h, c

def generate_caption(self,features,max_len=20,vocab=None):

    batch_size = features.size(0)
    h, c = self.init_hidden_state(features)

    #starting input
    word = torch.tensor(vocab.word2idx['<start>']).view(1,-1).cuda()
    embeds = self.embedding(word)

    captions = []
    for i in range(max_len):
        _,context = self.attention(features, h)

        lstm_input = torch.cat((embeds[:, 0], context), dim=1)
        output, c = self.lstm_cell(lstm_input, (h, c))
        output = self.fcn(self.drop(output))
        output = output.view(batch_size,-1)

        #select the word with most prob
        predicted_word_idx = output.argmax(dim=1)
        #save the generated word
        captions.append(predicted_word_idx.item())
        #end if <end> detected
        if vocab.idx2word[predicted_word_idx.item()] == "<end>":
            break
        #send generated word as the next caption
        embeds = self.embedding(predicted_word_idx.unsqueeze(0))

    #covert the vocab idx to words and return sentence
    return [vocab.idx2word[idx] for idx in captions]
```

FIGURE 9.14 The "forward", "init_hidden_state", and "generate_caption" methods for using LSTM with an attention mechanism.

```
class EncoderDecoder(nn.Module):
    def __init__(self,embed_size, vocab_size, attention_dim,encoder_dim,decoder_dim):
        super().__init__()
        self.encoder = EncoderCNN()
        self.decoder = DecoderRNN(
            embed_size=embed_size,
            vocab_size = len(vocab),
            attention_dim=attention_dim,
            encoder_dim=encoder_dim,
            decoder_dim=decoder_dim
        )

    def forward(self, images, captions):
        features = self.encoder(images)
        outputs = self.decoder(features, captions)
        return outputs
```

FIGURE 9.15 The "EncoderDecoder" class to combine the encoder and decoder into a model.

```
# Train & Validate
model = EncoderDecoder(
    embed_size=256,
    vocab_size = len(vocab),
    attention_dim=256,
    encoder_dim=2048,
    decoder_dim=512
)
model = nn.DataParallel(model)
model = model.cuda()
criterion = nn.CrossEntropyLoss(ignore_index=vocab.word2idx["<pad>"])

# for param in model.parameters():
#     param.requires_grad = True

from torch import optim
optimizer = optim.Adam(model.parameters(), lr=config.lr)
scheduler = optim.lr_scheduler.StepLR(optimizer,step_size=10,gamma=0.5)
```

FIGURE 9.16 Defining the model as "EncoderDecoder", importing "optim", and defining loss function, optimizer, and scheduler.

training images to the encoder to get features and passes the features to get captions as output. In the "EncoderDecoder" model encoder dimension is set to 2048 for using the ResNet50 model. The decoder dimension can be changed since it is newly defined (e.g., decoder_dim = 256 can be used).

Now, we implement cross-entropy loss as a criterion. It ignores pads in the captions during loss calculations. The "optim" is imported to implement different optimization algorithms and the "torchvision" module is utilized to access various model architectures and weights [8]. The Adam optimizer is defined using model parameters and learning rate. The

"StepLR" scheduler is used with 10 step size and a multiplicative factor of 0.5 to reduce the learning rate by half after 10 epochs.

It is recommended to launch Spyder IDE from "Anacoda Prompt" by entering the command "spyder" and running each of the program sections separately or line by line. For example, to run a section of the program in Spyder IDE (Windows), we may select multiple lines of code and press the "F9" button. This process will help the user to understand the codes step-by-step and pinpoint an error quickly. This case study example uses two GPUs (GeForce RTX 3090) with data parallelism to split the batches.

9.7 MODEL TRAINING AND SAVING THE BEST MODEL

Now the model is ready for training. A nested "for loop" is used to run the training for a number of epochs set by the default configurations ("config. epochs"). In this case study, the model is going to run for 15 epochs. Figure 9.17 shows the code for training the model and calculating loss in every iteration. A "step_check" variable is created to check and save the best model four times in an epoch. Initially, the best loss is set to a very large number (np.inf), and after every iteration, the program updates this best loss if a lower validation loss value is found. For this image captioning problem, training loss is defined by criterion in Figure 9.16 (i.e., cross-entropy loss). The "torch.cuda.empty_cache()" is used before training to release all unoccupied cashed memory for effective GPU operation. The code for this training process and printing the epoch numbers, training loss, and validation loss are shown in Figure 9.17.

The model training may return the "OutOfMemoryError: CUDA out of memory" error, which is an issue of GPU memory limitations. In that situation, the code won't execute, but we can resolve this problem by reducing the batch size or image size. Sometimes, restarting the kernel in the Spyder console may solve the out-of-memory issue. Compared to other case studies of this book, image captioning requires a significant amount of time (e.g., about five hours in our system).

Once the model runs and starts to train, we get a minimum validation loss of 3.485 after 11 epochs (Figure 9.18). In this case study, the training and validation datasets are randomly splitted, where the allocated training and validation images are 80% and 20% of the total images, respectively. In some machine learning practices, the total dataset is divided into three different categories: training, validation, and testing. Although both

```
best_loss= np.inf
steps = 0
step_check = int(len(train_loader)/4)
torch.cuda.empty_cache()
for epoch in range(config.epochs):
    train_loss = 0
    model.train()
    for (images, captions, lengths) in train_loader:
        images = images.cuda()
        captions = captions.cuda()
        outputs = model(images, captions)

        targets = captions[:,1:]
        loss = criterion(outputs.view(-1, len(vocab)), targets.reshape(-1))

        optimizer.zero_grad()
        loss.backward()
        optimizer.step()

        train_loss += loss.item()
        steps += 1

        if steps % step_check == 0:
            model.eval()
            valid_loss = 0
            with torch.no_grad():
                for (images, captions, lengths) in val_loader:
                    images = images.cuda()
                    captions = captions.cuda()
                    outputs = model(images, captions)

                    targets = captions[:,1:]
                    loss = criterion(outputs.view(-1, len(vocab)), targets.reshape(-1))

                    valid_loss += loss.item()
            if valid_loss < best_loss:
                best_loss = valid_loss
                print('saving model...')
                torch.save(model, config.data_dir+'/model.pt')

            print("Epoch: {}/{}.. ".format(epoch+1, config.epochs),
                  "Training Loss: {:.3f}.. ".format(train_loss/step_check),
                  "Validation Loss: {:.3f}.. ".format(valid_loss/len(val_loader)))

            model.train()
            train_loss = 0
    scheduler.step()

print("Finish")
```

FIGURE 9.17   Model training and saving the best model, and printing training and validation losses.

validation and testing datasets can be used interchangeably, in some cases, for unbiased evaluation of the model, the validation dataset may be utilized for early stopping in overfitting scenarios [9]. During training, if we find the best training loss within the first one or two epochs and after that loss increases randomly, the training should be terminated as it indicates that the model is failing to generalize the dataset and is overfitting.

```
Epoch: 11/15.. Training Loss: 2.551.. Validation Loss: 3.496..
Epoch: 11/15.. Training Loss: 2.579.. Validation Loss: 3.489..
saving model...
Epoch: 11/15.. Training Loss: 2.588.. Validation Loss: 3.485..
Epoch: 12/15.. Training Loss: 0.826.. Validation Loss: 3.494..
Epoch: 12/15.. Training Loss: 2.436.. Validation Loss: 3.502..
Epoch: 12/15.. Training Loss: 2.490.. Validation Loss: 3.499..
Epoch: 12/15.. Training Loss: 2.530.. Validation Loss: 3.490..
Epoch: 13/15.. Training Loss: 0.670.. Validation Loss: 3.502..
Epoch: 13/15.. Training Loss: 2.393.. Validation Loss: 3.518..
Epoch: 13/15.. Training Loss: 2.419.. Validation Loss: 3.520..
Epoch: 13/15.. Training Loss: 2.438.. Validation Loss: 3.507..
Epoch: 14/15.. Training Loss: 0.509.. Validation Loss: 3.521..
Epoch: 14/15.. Training Loss: 2.325.. Validation Loss: 3.525..
Epoch: 14/15.. Training Loss: 2.347.. Validation Loss: 3.517..
Epoch: 14/15.. Training Loss: 2.398.. Validation Loss: 3.514..
Epoch: 15/15.. Training Loss: 0.363.. Validation Loss: 3.529..
Epoch: 15/15.. Training Loss: 2.248.. Validation Loss: 3.539..
Epoch: 15/15.. Training Loss: 2.287.. Validation Loss: 3.524..
Epoch: 15/15.. Training Loss: 2.312.. Validation Loss: 3.541..
Finish
```

FIGURE 9.18 "Training Loss" is 2.588 and the best "Validation Loss" is 3.485 after 11 epochs.

9.8 MODEL TESTING AND INFERENCE

We may test the model performance by using images from the dataset manually. Figure 9.19 shows the code required to load the trained model from "model_path", and generate a caption for an image from the validation loader batch. The "features" and "caps" get the encoder and decoder from the DataParallel object using the module, respectively. The program will output a joined caption and corresponding image (Figure 9.19).

FIGURE 9.19 Load the trained model from "model_path", and plot the image and generated caption.

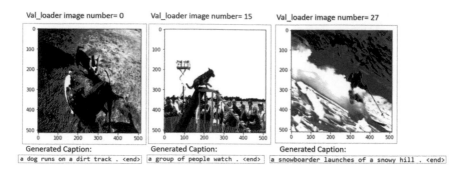

FIGURE 9.20   Caption generation using trained model and validation images.

We have checked several other images from the validation loader. For most of the images, generated captions are not perfect. However, the model can capture salient features of an image to some degree. Figure 9.20 shows three images from the validation batch (image index 0, 15, and 27) and generated captions. In image 15, we can see that the model can tell that a group of people are watching but fails to tell about the dog that they are watching. We could say that the model needs more fine-tuning and training for better predictions. One obstacle to fine-tuning the model is that it is relatively time-consuming to run.

Now we do the model inference using entirely new images in the real-world context. To test this, four different open-source pictures are downloaded from https://unsplash.com/. These pictures are renamed (e.g., Test1. jpg, Test2.jpg, Test3.jpg, and Test4.jpg) and available in the additional resources of this chapter. In our workstation, the images are saved into the Desktop's "Image_Captioning" Folder, as shown in Figure 9.21. The inference images are normalized, resized, and processed for caption generation. Figure 9.21 shows the program code required for model inference for "Test1.jpg".

Figure 9.22 demonstrates the image captioning for three other test images. In "Test1.jpg", the model can generate a caption reasonably well (Figure 9.21). It predicts that it is a dog running through the water. One possible reason for this result is that there was a good amount of dog activity and water pictures in the dataset. However, predictions for "Test2.jpg" and "Test4.jpg" don't show good results. Especially, in the "Test4.jpg", the model says a person is flying kites. This may be a reason for dataset limitations and can be improved by providing images of planes flying and describing them for the training.

```
img = cv2.imread(r"C:\Users\tariqarif\Desktop\Image_Captioning" +"/"+ "Test1.jpg")
img = cv2.cvtColor(img, cv2.COLOR_BGR2RGB)
img = img/255.0
img = cv2.resize(img,(config.img_width,config.img_height))
img = T.Compose([T.ToTensor(), T.Normalize(mean, std)])(img.copy())
img = img.unsqueeze(0).float().cuda()
features = model.module.encoder(img)
caps = model.module.decoder.generate_caption(features,vocab=vocab)
caption = ' '.join(caps)
print(caption)

img = img.squeeze(0)
img = img.permute(1,2,0).cpu().numpy()
plt.imshow(img)
```

Image: Test1.jpg

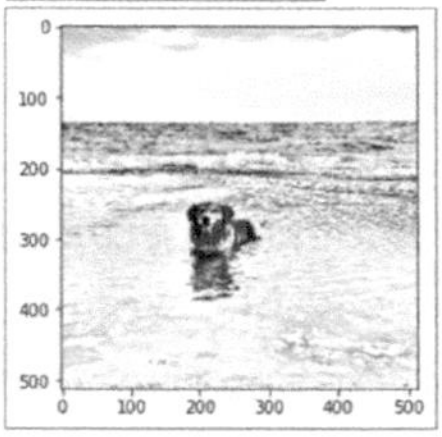

Generated Caption:

a dog is running through the water . <end>

FIGURE 9.21 Model inference using test images downloaded from online.

Generated Captions:

Image: Test2.jpg

a black dog jumps for a black dog jumps for a black dog jumps for a black dog jumps for

Image: Test3.jpg

a man is performing a yellow bike . <end>

Image: Test4.jpg

a person is flying kites . <end>

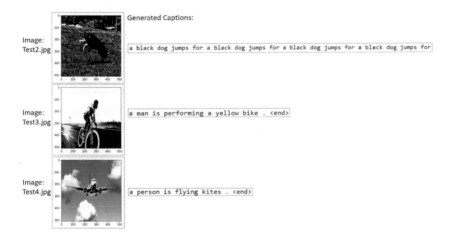

FIGURE 9.22 Model inference using downloaded images "Test2.jpg", "Test3.jpg", and "Test4.jpg".

9.8.1 Fine Tuning

For finding the optimal set of parameters, it is recommended to tweak different parameters and evaluate the outputs that minimize the loss and improve training/inference time. The codes given for this chapter can be updated by changing batch size, epochs, learning rate, optimizer,

```
import pandas as pd
caption_df = pd.read_csv(f'{config.data_dir}'+"/flickr8k/captions.csv")

###take one random caption per image
image_ids = [i for i in caption_df['image'].unique()]
captions = []
for i in image_ids:
    captions.append(caption_df.loc[caption_df['image']==i]['caption'].iloc[random.randint(0, 4)])
df = pd.DataFrame({'image':image_ids,'caption':captions})

#############
from sklearn.model_selection import train_test_split
train_data_list,valid_data_list = train_test_split(caption_df,test_size = 0.2,random_state = config.seed+1)
train_data_list,valid_data_list = train_test_split(df,test_size = 0.2,random_state = config.seed+1)
```

FIGURE 9.23   Remove "df" in the "train_test_split" that uses random captions and replace it with "caption_df".

schedulers, etc. For the common hyperparameter tuning, refer to Sections 6.9.1 and 6.9.2 from Chapter 6 and its exercises. One critical hyperparameter for this case study is the learning rate. In this example, we used a learning rate of 0.001. However, a small change in this learning rate significantly affects the learning process. The model tends to overfit very quickly with too big or small learning rates. For better results, the learning rate should be tuned along with "step_size" and "gamma". We may use different types of pre-trained CNN models and loss functions, as shown in the fine-tuning section of Chapters 7 and 8.

The model can also be tuned by altering how it reads captions for an image during training. In Figure 9.4, we have used one of the random captions out of five for the model training. If we want to include all of the captions for the training process, it will also change the training performance. However, the calculation time in this case would be much higher. Figure 9.23 shows the changes that need to be made in the program to use all of the captions for training.

The data frame "df" uses a random caption for training, and it can be updated to "caption_df" in the "train_test_split" (Figure 9.4).

Finally, the model can also be improved significantly by including more image data and corresponding captions for training.

9.9 SIMILAR APPLICATIONS FOR ENGINEERS

This chapter presents a case study of the image captioning problem using deep learning. The image dataset used here is freely available on Kaggel's site, and it is highly recommended that readers of this book try running the model using the same dataset. In the engineering fields, image captioning has numerous practical applications. For example, this technology can be used to assist very elderly or visually impaired people by describing a scene or environment. It can be used in security and surveillance applications to generate descriptions of unusual activities. In autonomous driving, images from video frames can be used to interpret less visible but dangerous areas to the passengers and aid in the decision-making process. Besides these potential applications, image captioning is currently heavily used in many social media and E-commerce platforms for better describing activities, events, or products. Although this technology has many limitations, it is expected to become more and more user-friendly in many commercial applications.

The following section presents image captioning model programming questions related to using training data differently and tweaking the model for fine-tuning.

9.10 EXERCISE PROBLEM

1. This chapter demonstrates an image captioning case study using the open-source Flickr 8k dataset. For the training process, it uses one random caption for an image. However, Section 9.9 discusses how can we use all the captions for model training. Implement all the captions for model training in the case study program and compare the model performance after 15 epochs.

2. Run the case study program for 5 epochs by reducing the learning rate to 0.0001. How this reduced learning rate is effecting the model performance?

3. In the case study program, change the image width and height to 1024 and reduce the batch size to 16. Comment on the model performance after 10 epochs.

REFERENCES

1. Persson, A., 2020, "Flickr8k-Images-Captions," https://www.kaggle.com/datasets/aladdinpersson/flickr8kimagescaptions.
2. Bird, S., Klein, E., and Loper, E., 2009, Natural Language Processing with Python, O'Reilly Media, Inc., ISBN: 9780596516499.
3. PyTorch, 2023 "Transforming and augmenting images," https://pytorch.org/vision/stable/transforms.html.
4. Bradski, G., 2000, "The openCV Library," Dr. Dobb's Journal: Software Tools for the Professional Programmer, 25(11), pp. 120–123.
5. imgaug, 2020, "Overview of Augmenters.", https://imgaug.readthedocs.io/en/latest/source/overview_of_augmenters.html

6. 2023, "Transforming and augmenting images," https://pytorch.org/vision/stable/transforms.html#torchvision.transforms.ToTensor.
7. 2023, "Torch.utils.data," https://pytorch.org/docs/stable/data.html.
8. 2023, "PyTorch torch.optim," https://pytorch.org/docs/stable/optim.html.
9. Prechelt, L., 2012, "Early Stopping—But When?," Neural Networks: Tricks of the Trade: 2nd Ed., G. Montavon, G. B. Orr, and K.-R. Müller, eds., Springer, Berlin Heidelberg, pp. 53–67.

Index

Note: Page numbers in *italics* indicate a figure.